Crossing the Frontier

Stories and Poems by Senior Writers
Elkhart and St. Joseph Counties, Indiana

Crossing the Frontier

Stories and Poems by Senior Writers
Elkhart and St. Joseph Counties, Indiana

Editor
John Bender

Book design
Sarah Herr

Artwork
Contributed by writers and visual artists

GREENCROFT  COMMUNITIES

Acknowledgments:
Cover: Watercolor painting by Martha K. Pigors, a resident of Greencroft Goshen.
Subject: "My mother, Ellen, sister Laura (left) and me. Done from a snapshot
taken about 1915 in Chicago's Grant Park." Born in 1914 and growing up in
Chicago, Mrs. Pigors took art classes in elementary school, and all through high
school at the Art Institute of Chicago. "I fell out of my cradle with a crayon in my
hand."
Back cover: Multimedia art by Areta G. Lehman, Tea Country (p. 115).

Library of Congress Control Number: 2008921290

ISBN-10: 1-933858-35-4
ISBN-13: 978-1-933858-35-7

Printed in the United States of America

Provided with support through the Elkhart County Community Foundation,
Elkhart, Ind.; the Community Foundation of St. Joseph County by the Indiana
Arts Commission, a state agency; and the National Endowment for the Arts, a
federal agency.

Dedicated to the senior writers whose work inspires, informs and entertains people of all ages.

Contents

Part Three

Foreword

The poems and essays in this book come from the heart. The heart does not lie. These stories reveal writers' personal encounters with others, with themselves, with nature. They bubble up from memories of childhood and youth, as newlyweds, as singles, as extended family. *Crossing the Frontier* reflects insights, wisdom and humor born of experience. The stories tell of life transitions, of dangers and losses, coping, community celebrations, grace-filled awakenings, new pursuits.

A line from the poem by Helen Alderfer, "Old Age," brings to mind the purposeful yet far-reaching view of what living can mean for older adults: "Remember, you are a pioneer with a frontier to be crossed."

Many older adults are experiencing a new sense of freedom as they graduate from fixed roles in family, career and community. Older adults enter that stage of life where they can explore new creative pursuits, focus on spirituality, attend to grandchildren or grandnieces and nephews, give thought to the legacy they are leaving, make time for old and new friends, create a new sense of home in a changed living environment, find joy, peace and purpose by leaving the world a better place . . . possibly through the sharing of their stories.

Even with feet planted solidly in the present, the writers in this volume also share their hope and insight into the natural progression from this life to the next.

Writers were encouraged to focus on one event or happening that gave meaning to their life: "Share a telling incident from the people, places or occurrences related to your family or ancestors, or wider relationships with people and nature. What happened that changed the direction of your life? What was the greatest challenge you faced? What do you want your great-grandchildren to know? What spiritual experience influenced your life? What is the funniest, saddest or best thing that has happened to you? What has helped you cope with a current situation?"

Writers were encouraged to avoid the temptation in writing to "preach," or try to make sure they get some great "learning" across. The best stories or poems, the guidelines noted, "are those that let the images speak for themselves, to illuminate or enlighten, that let us 'live the experience and the learning,' but which avoid making the point too directly."

Some of the writers sharpened their writing skills through a four-session course offered in spring 2007 by The Lifelong Learning Institute of Elkhart County and a writing course offered at Greencroft Senior Center, Goshen. Some have been writing for a long time and others are just getting started in the craft. In an effort to accommodate as many entries as possible in this first time writing contest, we invited essays of up to 800 words and poems of up to 40 lines. Those entries that exceeded the guidelines were not considered for the prize competition, however, with some abbreviation, they too are included in this volume.

Greencroft Communities is pleased to have had a hand in bringing the creativity and insights of these writers to a wider audience. One goal of the writing project was to have older adults share their stories not only with each other but with another generation. With the generous financial support from the Indiana Arts Commission through The Community Foundation of St. Joseph County, from the Elkhart County Community Foundation and from Wal-Mart Stores, a quantity of books was made available to sophomore students at Goshen High School and to residents of the Greencroft Communities in Elkhart and St. Joseph Counties, Indiana. Each writer received free copies for themselves and their families. The project also proposed having some of the writers read their poems and essays at area libraries and senior centers.

Sharing these stories with all their heart shows the important role that storytellers and knowledge-keepers have in society. Words are power. May these writers touch your heart, too. Thank you to each of the writers who share their story here:

Essay first place, Paton Yoder, "Good Night"; second place, Ginny Welker, "You Have a Beautiful Smile"; third place, Pat Clark, "Making Music with Marshal."

Other essay writers selected for publication, in alphabetical order, include: Bertha Beachy, Carol Bogol, Mabel Brunk, Miriam Charles, Jean Crist, Robert Edwards Sr., Rosemary Blosser Fry, Weyburn Groff, Elizabeth Hernley, Marie S. Hoey, Martha Huebert, Bobbie Lee Hudson, Janet Elliott Hughey, Martini Reimer Janz, Helen Kennell, Betty A. Kidd, Karen Leigh (Robertson), Ruth Conrad Liechty, Roseanna Foley Maust, Mary Elizabeth Martucci, Jack McKeever, Patricia McKinney, Lora Miranda, Millie Myers, Florence Nafziger, Laverne Nafziger, Tillie Nauraine, Marjorie Banman Neufeld, Lena Poindexter, Daniel Roll, Phillip C. Ross, M. J. Richardson, Paula Stoltzfus, Reynold Sawatzky, David A. Shank, Wilma Edith Hollopeter Shank, Kathryn Steckly, Lois R. Stickel, Ethel

Stutzman Arlie Waggy, Naomi Waggy, Gerry Warstler, Esther B. Yoder and Gladys O. (DuMond) Zimmerman.

Poetry first place, Helen Alderfer, "Old Age"; second place, Verna Birky, "Ode to the Pacific"; third place, Areta G. Lehman, "Tea Country."

Other poetry writers selected for publication, in alphabetical order, include: Hope Bartlett, Royal Bauer, Luke Birky, Nadine (Hoke) Corse, Georgia A. Gill Elkins, Sandra A. Fryer, Doreen Geary, Chuck Hernley, Laurence M. Horst, Katherine Johnson, Lola Kauffmann, Lila Miller, Betty Muhlnickel, Sandra Neilson, and Erma Yoder.

Thanks to Shari Wagner (poetry) and Leonard Beechy (essays) who judged the original entries and then gave suggestions for revisions. Thanks to Karen Ritchie for expert copy editing, to Tracy Bishop for editorial help, and others who read the manuscript and made suggestions. The Senior Writing Contest Committee included Jennifer Hayes (chair), John Bender, Cathy Beery Berg, Dina Harris, Rochelle Hurt, Matthew Lentsch and Kelly Schrock.

I take responsibility for any errors that, for reasons all too human, too often find their way into print. I ask forbearance, trusting that readers and writers will keep right on reading and writing.

John Bender
November 2007

Director of Public Relations
Greencroft Communities
(Retired, January 2008)

Introduction

Living now is what the writers in this book of essays and poems are doing. Their stories come from the heart. Some will make you laugh, some will bring tears to your eyes, most will make you reflect on your own experiences and relationships growing up or in your adult years.

If these stories take you into new or renewed areas of reflection, it is because the writers cared about sharing what was on their hearts. If you are inspired to do likewise, do it! If you've already written your story, share it with all who are dear to you. You are an affirming presence among all those with whom you interact.

I need not recite statistics of the aging global population or comment on the significance of changing demographics on economic and social spheres. I need not tell you how to take care of yourself through a healthy diet, exercise and active social life. I need not tell you that life has challenges as well as opportunities for people to live fully in their senior years.

I will tell readers young and old alike, to look for the stories of our elders. I will tell elders to share from all their heart as they join a host of others on a pioneer trek across a new frontier. Space or time travel holds no candle to the stories older adults have to tell.

Mark King
President and Chief Executive Officer

Greencroft Communities

Part 1: Essays

Good Night
Paton Yoder

October 31, 2006, 2007 or even 2008 . . . in any case, it's the autumn of our lives and it's evening. Hazel and I are sitting on this convenient park bench along the road leading out of town.

We came into town this morning and I got a job and Mother soon had one, too. Hers included taking care of our five children and other responsibilities. It has been a pleasant day. In spite of some irresponsible and reprehensible mistakes as we tried to do our respective jobs, we felt – and still feel – that we were working for the Lord. That conviction gave purpose and pleasure to our busy lives. That was way back 94 years ago when we came into town.

It has been a long day. We were rather tired when we plunked ourselves down on this park bench at quitting time. But now we've been sitting here for 20-some years and are quite well rested up.

We've enjoyed this rest. We've been teasing and tormenting each other as we sat here like we've never had time for during our working days. When we weren't teasing each other, we were watching the cars and buses go by. Oh, we got some pleasure helping a couple of drivers change tires, and in giving directions to tourists who were lost. And several times, Hazel was able to slip a carton of milk to a mother with a crying child. But much of the time we just sat.

The traffic has been heavy all evening. A bus with my brother, among others, soon came by. And then there were still more who were leaving – relatives and friends. They were headed out of town and the buses were crowded. They seemed to be in a hurry and only cried out "good-bye" to us as they disappeared down the street. I understand they were headed for heaven. Then came those few of our friends who had stayed at their jobs a little longer than we had. All during this evening hour, our children and grandchildren were bringing us blankets and soda pop and other supplies as the hours accumulated. They wanted to make certain that we were warm and comfortable. I never drank so much Mountain Dew before in my entire life!

The sun has now dropped out of sight in the West and the shadows are giving way to the gathering darkness. Here we sit on this roadside bench on the outskirts of town, dangling our feet and legs like little children waiting for their school bus. We've had a pleasant evening, just lounging on this park bench and gently tormenting each other and watching the world go by, basking in God's love, waiting for our bus. But it's getting a little tedious and quiet. Soon it will become rather chilly. I never like the cold. And I'm getting a little fidgety. I'd rather not wait much longer.

I wonder when our bus will come by to pick us up? Will we both be able to get on the same one? It would be sad, indeed, for either of us to sit here into the night all alone, waiting for the next bus. But even if that turns out to be the case, there remains the prospect of a bright eternity in the morning.

First place
Judge's comment: I'm a great admirer of this piece. It shows what can be done in a brief space with artistry, wisdom and a poetic, figurative sensibility. It takes a stage of life and offers the reader, as some poems do, the sense that it "says it all."

You Have a Beautiful Smile
Ginny Welker

"Ma'am," he said. "I hope you don't take this in the wrong way, but you have a beautiful smile."

He spoke quietly. He did not wink or grin broadly. He had not tried to engage in superficial conversation. He was not flirtatious, arrogant or pompous as were many of the men who came into our office. He was clean and neat, a gentleman in every way. He had come for assistance with the aerial maps our office kept. I had helped him, but before he turned to go, he spoke those simple words.

"Ma'am," he said, "you have a beautiful smile."

His sincere compliment fell as healing oil on my wounded spirit. I was broken, frightened and withdrawn. Having just left a 28-year marriage filled with mental, emotional and physical abuse, I feared all men. This was my first job outside the home in nearly 24 years. I learned the work well, but waiting on men caused my hands to shake, my body to perspire, and my mind to go blank. I was vulnerable and, oh, so fragile. But then I heard his encouraging words.

"Ma'am," he said, "you have a beautiful smile."

My mother had taught me to smile. "When you don't know what to say, you need not say a word. A smile is enough," she advised. Or, "When in adult company, you should smile quietly and wait to be addressed before speaking." As I approached the awkward teenage years, her wisdom spoke again: "When you're having a bad-hair day, smile cheerfully and no one will notice your hair." As I grew older, my mother would encourage me to smile by reminding me, "You never know what others are going through as they pass by. A warm smile might be all they need to help them have a better day. Smiling is contagious; share yours with everyone you meet. One day, you'll be glad you did." Mom was right.

"Ma'am," he said, "you have a beautiful smile."

It was really all I had to give at this moment in my life. I could not have engaged in a friendly conversation. I could not have escorted him to the next office. I could not have given him a compliment or offered words of encouragement. I could only have given him what I had – a warm smile to greet him and send him on his way. Just as my mother had said many years before, on this particular day I was so glad that I had shared my smile with another, for in sowing a smile, I reaped words that have encouraged me to this day. I will always remember the healing that began to occur that day because one man took the effort to speak kindly to a broken woman.

"Ma'am," he said, "you have a beautiful smile."

Second place
By creating the first ever Greencroft Senior Adult Writing Contest you have made it possible for all of us aspiring writers to go beyond the spoken word as we surrender our hearts to paper. I am delighted! This story happened to me more than eight years ago, just a short time after I left the Elkhart County Women's Shelter. My mother was right. We never know when a simple kindness shown to another will return to us tenfold.

Judge's comment: You achieve a kind of poetry with your use of repetition and with the impressive account of yourself you're able to convey in a short piece. In my view, this is a very successful and effective piece.

Making Music with Marshal
Pat Clark

Doing what comes naturally. For some it is decorating a house, painting a picture, or cooking a delicious meal. How often do you say to someone, "I wish I could do that!" I've kept a secret close to my heart since I was a young girl. I have always wanted to be a concert pianist playing at Carnegie Hall in New York. Marshal, our Chocolate Lab, found his niche while just a puppy. It is making people happy.

From the day Marshal arrived in our house, he began changing our lives in a special way. One Saturday on our way home from the vet's clinic, I stopped to check on my aunt at a local nursing home. It was a cold, snowy day and I was concerned about leaving Marshal in the car. I asked permission to bring him in while I visited. This took longer than usual once people discovered I had a 5-month lab with me. Staff asked if the residents could see him. People suggested I bring him back the following weekend. A week later, I returned with Marshal to test the waters. We were greeted with outstretched arms and bright smiles from everyone. It was just like the first time we visited. On my next visit, I left him at home. It was then that I discovered it was the puppy they really wanted to see, not me. The staff shared stories about pets visiting the nursing home from time to time. They told me the residents enjoyed seeing Marshal. People began calling him "Marshal Mellow" and "Happy Dog" during our visits.

Growing quickly, Marshal was no longer a ball of fur, but a bundle of energy. He had a bit of magic about him that made him very special. His tail wagged to the left and shook to the right. He was the happiest puppy I've ever known. His smile could light up a street shrouded in clouds on a dark winter's night. Clearly, we were blessed with a dog that had a heart of gold and unconditional love for everyone he met. Having a lab in our home was like a daily dose of happiness energized with puppy breath. It soon became apparent we had to find an outlet for his electricity.

With summer around the corner, I began training him to walk on a leash in the cul-de-sac in front of our home. It was there that I met Anselm and Eva Fleithmann. These children would stop to play with Marshal after school. Soon they were regular visitors at our house. Playing ball in our backyard, taking Marshal for walks, and practicing obedience with him helped burn some of his energy. Yet, it seemed none of us could wear him out.

I had given a lot of thought to pet therapy and believed Marshal had potential to be a therapy dog. Could this be his mission in life? After several sessions of obedience classes and weekly visits to the nursing home, we earned certification as a TDI Pet Therapy Team with Therapy Dogs International Inc. Throughout Michiana we have visited hospitals, the Center for the Homeless, Madison Center, Juvenile Justice Center, schools, Sisters of the Holy Cross, and area nursing homes. It is amazing how much he loves these visits.

Marshal knows it is time to go to work when he sees me get out his Pet Therapy tote with his water bottle, toys, photo album, and special kerchiefs that delight the people he meets. Working as a therapy dog allows him to channel his strength in a positive way. Since starting his career in 2001, Marshal has earned three Pet Therapy endorsements: TDI, TDIA and TDIAOV, which appear after his name as a result of our work. These awards recognize him as an "Outstanding Volunteer Therapy" dog. Marshal even has his own business cards where he proudly displays the Canine Good Citizen and Pet Therapy titles he has earned.

Pet therapy is a two-way street. It offers those we visit the pleasure of petting and hugging a very patient dog who is willing to have a pat on the head, his ears stroked, his back scratched, or his belly rubbed by total strangers. Our visits allow me to hear many stores of treasured pets that gave those we met a lifetime of joyous memories. That is the two-way part of the street. Now when I hear, "There's Marshal," I know that is my way of being a concert pianist making music in the lives of those we touch. If you listen carefully, you, too, can hear the melody playing softly in the background.

Third place
Judges comment: This is an impressive piece of writing: Clear, enjoyable, energetic. The "music" theme is an unlikely unifying element, but I think it works beautifully. Congratulations on both this story and the music you and Marshal make.

The Universal Language
Mabel V. Brunk

In our small general hospital, the pediatric department is a wing of the adult division where I was working with nursing students one evening. During a lull in my activities, I heard continued crying coming from the pediatric ward and walked over to see if I could help.

The source of the crying was a golden haired youngster about 3 years old, huddled in the corner of a bed, looking unhappy and lonely. I sat down beside her and tried to start a conversation. The crying quieted to a soft whimper, but questions about her doll's name, whether it was sick, too, and if she would like to hear a story brought not even a nod of response and no change in the frightened look.

I decided to try a story anyway. Holding the book so the child could see the pictures, I started to read. At the end of the first story, she had stopped whimpering. At the end of the second, she had relaxed against the pillows, was clutching her doll less tensely, and freed one hand to copy my gesture of stroking the teddy bear in the picture. But still not even a nod or a shake of the head in response to any of my questions. I left her then, at last winning a shy smile as I waved good-bye.

Later that evening, I met the pediatric nurse on the elevator. "Thanks for reading to Linda; she hasn't cried since. You knew she didn't understand English, didn't you?" Seeing my surprised expression, she continued, "You see, her parents moved here from Norway and Linda was admitted this afternoon."

Real communication had occurred in what was outwardly a one-way conversation in a language foreign to the listener. Linda may not have understood English, but she did understand the universal language of friendliness in which words are subordinate to a sympathetic spirit.

After my "conversation" with Linda, I wondered how often my words have been phrased to express my sympathy, but the listener had not received the intended message because the spirit of compassion was lacking. I determined to become more proficient in the language of the understanding heart.

The Softer Side of Love
Marie S. Hoey

Papa was six feet tall with black curly hair; one curl rolled to one side like a small pompadour. His moustache covered his top lip and set off his fine features. His large, tanned, sinewy hands were gnarled and bruised from his years of labor on the railroad.

Papa had immigrated to America in the early 1900s. He came for all the same reasons so many flocked to this country. It was to be the fulfillment of the dream for a better life. But good jobs were scarce and most immigrants accepted any work available.

Shortly before the Depression years, Papa married. He continued to work hard, often long hours to provide for his growing family. I don't remember many hugs or caresses as a youngster, but, then, culture dictated parental roles in those days. Papa assumed the role of rough, tough, macho man and enjoyed his card-playing smokers with his buddies. Mama nurtured me and expressed her love where Papa seldom did. Somehow, though, I knew he loved me; his twinkling eyes and gentleness told me so.

This softer side of Papa became more apparent as he grew older. My first image of Papa communicating his feelings more openly was when he "babysat" our neighbor's 3-year-old. Every evening after supper, Papa sat out on the front steps, relaxing and enjoying the fresh air and chatting with the neighbors. In those days, no one had the luxury of air conditioning, and neighbors actually talked to one another.

One evening, the 3-year-old neighbor walked over to sit beside Papa. They chatted and after a while, they said good-bye. The same thing happened each night for a week. The next week I observed Papa lifting the child to his lap and they "read" a magazine together. Their visit lasted 20 minutes or more and when it was time to leave, Papa and the child kissed. I couldn't believe my eyes and could hardly wait for the next night's visit. The same thing happened when their visit ended, but this time I had my camera. I cherish that photo of Papa's expression of his softer side.

Some years later, I almost missed sharing a second incident, which had been going on for weeks. If I hadn't been home with a minor illness, I'd have missed it. I was in the kitchen making coffee when I heard a light tapping on the kitchen screen door. Papa was at the kitchen table having lunch so I answered the tapping. There on the back porch stood three little girls (ages 3, 4 and 5 years) who lived several houses away. The oldest one looked up and, somewhat surprised to see me, hesitated before asking, "Can Frank come out and play?"

My surprise gave way to laughter when I turned to Papa and saw the wide grin on his face. "They come over every afternoon," he said, adding, "We play cards and read books until nap time." My mouth dropped open with astonishment.

Papa never had any formal education, spoke some English, but not well, didn't play solitaire or other kids' card games! Obviously, his gentleness, patience and love was communicated despite these limitations. In the words of B.J. Hoff, "A father/grandfather expresses his love, not so much with his words, but in language that only the heart understands." That was Papa!

My only regret is that Papa never got to know his own grandchildren, or they, him. These images that I cherish, I take every opportunity to share with his grandchildren at family gatherings.

From Tragedy to Blessing
Gerry Warstler

It was a beautiful warm sunny day in March 1946 and my father and I were working at our old hardware store in northern Indiana. We loved to be at our old store with its wood floors that we oiled ever so often to keep it clean and settle the dust. There was a ladder that moved on a track in order to get the merchandise off the shelves that went to the ceiling. The store also had a balcony that it has to this day. Back then, there were horse collars hanging from the railing.

It was a nice Wednesday afternoon and a friend of my fathers came in the store and asked him if he would like to take a ride in his airplane. My father looked at me and asked, "Would you like to go?" Of course, in 1946, flying in an airplane was a great experience and I was very eager to go. I rode with our friend to the airport to get the plane and my father and sister went to the field a few miles north of town where we were to land.

While landing, the plane lost its altitude and it made a nosedive into the ground, falling about 1,000 feet. Both of us were critically injured, so two ambulances were called to take us to the hospital that was 15 miles away. I was bleeding very badly with many injuries—mostly broken bones, severe cuts and gashes. The pilot's injuries were more severe than mine, but not so evident as they were internal. He died seven hours later.

If this accident had happened today, we would have been airlifted to the nearest trauma center. But as it was, the doctor in the ER at the Elkhart Hospital had been a flight surgeon in the army and knew immediately what kind of accident he was dealing with. He told my parents he would give me a one in a hundred chance to live.

Prayers went up immediately and God was good to me. The nine weeks I was in the hospital was a time of surgeries and discomfort, but full of blessings. The caring friends and family were at my side constantly to encourage me and give me comfort. With both feet severely injured and a broken leg, I was confined to bed and a wheelchair all summer, but in seven months I learned to walk again.

Two years after the accident and recuperating from more surgery, a wonderful man came into my life. Out of the clear, blue sky, he came to our door and my mother invited him in. I had known him as a little boy, but the family had moved away. He came back to our area after being discharged from the army. My father needed help at the hardware store, so my friend was hired. It didn't take long until we knew we were meant for each other; we were married on Thanksgiving Day 1948.

After many years, we were able to purchase the store from my father. The store is in its 119th year and still doing well. As we look back on our lives, we know we are not promised a life free of pain and problems, but we are promised a caring God who walks with us every step of the way.

A Story for Rodney
Elizabeth Hernley

It was therapy time for our 4-year-old son, Rodney. The boys' club from our church was enjoying a baseball game in a field behind our country home. When I told our son it was time for his exercises, he pleaded, "Please, Mommy, let me stay until this inning is over." I readily agreed to

Rodney and sister, Ellen, in 1946.

the delay, realizing that our son could not participate in simple running games that most youngsters enjoy; he could be a spectator only.

Rodney had been born with multiple problems in his lower extremities: His hips were dislocated, he had no kneecaps, no movement in his ankles, and numerous ligaments needed surgery to lengthen them. At the age of 6 weeks he was in a body cast—encased rigidly from under his arms to the tips of his toes! From that age through the age of 14 years, he was in braces or casts almost constantly. We had determined early on, that if walking would be an impossibility for him, we'd remember his Aunt Miriam's response when she first saw his twisted legs: "If this child is never able to walk, we'll teach him to fly."

One of the early orthopedic surgeons to take Rod's case had advised: "Never do anything for this child that he can learn to do himself. When he falls, let him learn to get up himself. Many parents are too quick to help a child with a disability."

This same doctor also taught us the various exercises that would be included into the regular schedule. These should help to increase Rodney's ability to walk—and once he could walk better, they would improve his stance and stride. The exercises were to be done four times daily—and always for at least 30 minutes each time! The surgeon stated that these sessions would be painful for both the child and the mother. The stretching and exercising of joints and tendons HAD to hurt if they were to stretch beyond their present capability.

When I heard the clank of Rodney's braces on the porch outside, I readied myself by sitting in my usual chair for removing the braces. I wasn't prepared for Rodney's greeting. As he came through the door, he muttered through clenched teeth: "There's somebody I hate—and it's God!"

With my whole being I was praying—though no sentence formed or strength came to face this dilemma. I felt completely drained of energy for words. I found myself holding out my arms to this troubled child. When he was in his favorite position on my lap and I was unfastening his cumbersome leg braces, I heard myself say, "Roddy-boy, I have a story to tell you about the day you were born."

As I heard myself speaking so confidently, I wondered what on earth I was thinking. What would I say about that day? Our lives had changed drastically since then, and I wasn't sure I could remember correctly. I do know I prayed desperately for divine help. Soon, I was aware of my own voice telling stories about our family life that I hadn't thought about since our family began growing. Many details were omitted for a 4-year-old's understanding—I didn't want to complicate his life further.

Roddy, soon after you were born, while the nurses were getting you bathed and dressed, the doctor who delivered you came and sat by my bed. He told me that there seemed to be a problem with your legs and feet. He had never seen anything like this before, so he wanted a specialist to see you and advise him as to what should be done. He told us that he knew of an orthopedic surgeon in South Bend and with our consent would arrange an appointment as soon as possible. Your daddy had not arrived yet from camp in Pennsylvania so a friend offered to drive my mother and you, our precious baby, there at once.

While you were gone, a new patient was brought into my room and into another bed. This new mother was a 16-year-old and soon her doctor came in and sat beside her bed. She had given birth to her first child—a beautiful, healthy baby girl—the doctor said. Then the doctor continued: "We understand that you plan to put your baby up for adoption, so after you hold her awhile, we'll have some questions that must be answered before that can be legalized. And we'll need the signature of the father, so we'll need his name and where he can be contacted."

At the mention of the word "father," the young mother began protesting loudly: "Please Doctor Bender, just let me go home to my dog! I don't want to see the baby. Oh, please, just let me go home. My dog misses me so much and I miss my dog so much! I don't know the name of the father. There were some soldiers near the train station where some of us girls had just got off another train—we were told to be good to them because they were going to war for us. Please, I know my dog needs me."

As I finished quoting the young mother, I saw my 4-year-old was crying. In the midst of tears, he turned facing me as his arms tightened around my neck. "Oh, Mommy," he sobbed, "I'm so glad God gave me to you and Daddy instead of that woman!"

Rodney did learn to walk. Even though the exercises still hurt, this story helped him have a more accepting attitude.

You Saved the Family
Martha Huebert

Martha (Mardy), left, with her mother, sister Elsie and brother Billy stand in front of their home on 122 Street, Harlem, N.Y., 1949 or 1950.

At her 90th birthday party, shortly before she started showing signs of dementia, Mom said to me, "I feel so bad that you and Elsie had to go to work so young."

"We never resented it," I answered, "We were glad to help out."

"You did much more than help out," Mom said, "You saved the family!"

It was in 1954, and I was 15-years-old. My parents, immigrants from Germany, were struggling to bring up three children in Harlem, a run-down section of New York City. Just a few days earlier, my 16-year-old sister had been followed into the long dark, narrow hallway of our apartment. A man grabbed her on the stairway, but her screams and other people coming out of their apartments had chased him away.

A family council was held. "We've got to move away from here," Mom said. "Elsie and Mardy are growing up in fear. Who knows what could happen to them? And Billy starts junior high in September and will have to go to that awful school, with gangs, weapons and violence."

"What can we do?" Dad answered bitterly. "Even with all of the overtime at the factory, and your school crossing job, we can just barely pay the low rent here."

"I've been looking around," Mom answered. "There's a nice apartment available just over the bridge in Astoria—but it costs almost twice as much as this one."

"What about us?" I cried out. "Elsie and I have our part-time jobs at Woolworth's, and if we take on a few extra afternoons, and give you all our pay, we can afford the move! We have to get out of here."

"All our friends have already moved to the Bronx or Queens, where there are trees, lawns, back yards!" Elsie added.

We all sat around the large oval table in the cramped living room while dad added up the figures. Finally, he decided. "If you two girls could contribute your salaries to the rent money, we could move. But I don't want to see your schoolwork suffer because of it. A good education is more important than a nice neighborhood!"

We eagerly agreed to continue doing our homework and keeping up our good grades, even while working four afternoons and Saturdays at Woolworth's instead of only Saturdays. We consulted our boss, who was only too happy to give us the extra hours.

And so one sunny day our furniture was packed onto the back of a truck and we went over the Triboro Bridge to 32nd Street, Astoria, Queens. The apartment was on the top floor of a three-family house. There were trees in the front yard, and a lawn where Billy could play ball with his new friends. Sunlight streamed through the large windows. It didn't matter that the elevated trains thundered past our windows every few minutes, day and night. We had escaped—and now lived in a beautiful apartment where we no longer had to be afraid to walk home at night.

Now, 50 years later, Mom was apologizing for "making us go to work so young."

"Mom, you are wrong. It was the best thing that ever happened to us. We learned that our contribution, our work and our money, were valuable to the family. We grew up that day. We learned responsibility. We learned that together we are stronger. And we had a chance to thank you for being wonderful parents."

Mom has dementia now. She doesn't remember the recent past, and even the far-off past is receding. She doesn't remember that all three of her children are college graduates. But one thing none of us has ever forgotten—we are a family, we stick together.

My Trip to Boston – July 2007
Millie Myers

When I picked up a brochure announcing a bus tour to Boston, I thought it would be fun to go to Boston by bus and see my youngest daughter, Becki, her husband, Phil, and sons, Troy 14, and Bryce, 8. The Holiday Inn at Woburn was just around the corner from their home.

Sunday afternoon we arrived at the Holiday Inn at Niagara Falls. Another half-full bus arrived and we all went to a restaurant for supper. After supper, quite a few of the people took a walk to see the Falls. I chose to go back to the hotel.

Monday morning we left for Lockport, N.Y., where we picked up 30 more seniors. We arrived in Boston around 4:00 p.m.

I decided to skip most of the activities that were planned for the tour so that I could be with Becki and her family. They picked me up and we ate out. They then came up to my room and visited for about an hour.

Tuesday morning, Phil picked me up about 9:30 and we went to their home. That first morning was spent talking about genealogy. My genealogy is complicated, so Troy wrote everything on a white board to be transposed to paper later. They wanted to know how it happened that I went to four high schools and also about the Kansas City, Mo. Voluntary Service unit where my husband and I got acquainted.

After lunch, Troy and Bryce played the keyboard for awhile. They also got out their Game Boys and played with them. I got on the computer and read 57 of my emails.

For supper we had pizza and chocolate pie. That is what they get to celebrate. Phil took me back to the hotel about 9:00 and insisted on walking up to my room.

My roommate came in very tired at 11:30 p.m. They had been gone since 8:00 a.m. that morning; they had been in and out of the bus quite a few times, and the ground was rough where they went to hear the Boston Pops Orchestra. I was so glad I hadn't been with them.

Wednesday morning, Troy and Bryce came with Phil when he picked me up. We played Chinese checkers, talked, and watched TV.

Phil was going to get some meat to grill, but I told them I was planning to see the fireworks with the coach group so I wouldn't be there for supper. We had the rest of the yummy pizza and chocolate pie for lunch.

Thursday morning while we were eating breakfast, Becki, Troy and Bryce came to the hotel to say good-bye. The boys agreed to write to me the first of the month and I will write after mid-month to keep in touch.

Then we left for Lockport, N.Y., where we left the 30 we had picked up, ate supper at a restaurant, and stayed at another Holiday Inn.

We enjoyed a hot breakfast of scrambled eggs, potatoes, sausage and bacon. The breakfasts in Boston were good, but cold. We left for Goshen at 8:00 a.m. and I walked into my apartment at 5:30 p.m. Friday evening—exactly the time they said we would be home.

Our driver told us we had driven more than 2,000 miles. I had a wonderful time! I learned to know new people—whose names I don't remember. The weather was fantastic, and I thoroughly enjoyed spending time with my Massachusetts family for a couple of days.

A week later, I had breakfast with my two Goshen daughters, Lynda and Beth. Although we live hundreds of miles apart, it was great to feel as if I had just seen and talked with my three daughters.

The Grand Canyon Challenges
Arlie Waggy

After finding a sleeping room, my wife, Naomi, said, "Let's go out and take a look at the Canyon before we go to bed." We saw first, not the Canyon, but a dozen youth standing on an overlook holding hands toward the sky. When I asked them what was going on, one said, "Touch me and see." I did, and received a strong electrical shock. There was a storm in the Canyon and they were receiving electrical charges from electrostatic activity in the clouds. Just about two weeks before, I had read of two youth getting caught in a thunderstorm in the Grand Tetons and they were burned, especially under their belt buckles. I was a little leery about participating in their fun.

However, I soon discovered that no sky-pointing was necessary. All I needed to get charged was to stand in there. Then to get discharged, and shocked, I could touch the iron railing around the overlook or touch another person. No one seemed to be getting damaged.

See girl's fine hair standing up Also, boy's small tuft in center, all of which are electrostatically charged.

A visit to the Grand Canyon in 1971 created more than one hair-raising experience for the Waggy family. Here, atmospheric conditions are raising Arlie's and two bystanders' hair electrostatically.

The next day was sunny, and my 14-year-old son, Loren, and I hiked the Kaibab Trail about 10 km (6.2 miles) down to the Colorado River, crossed on a footbridge, and hiked up the north side of the Canyon to Phantom Ranch for sandwiches and apples for lunch.

After lunch, we walked down the Colorado River, crossed it on a different footbridge, and started up Bright Angel Trail. I stopped to use a ramshackle outdoor toilet. When I came out, Loren had his shoes off and was sitting in the hot sun, soaking his feet in a little warm stream coming down from Indian Gardens on Bright Angel Trail. By 1:00 p.m., we had walked a lot, and the temperature was about 110° F, so even warm water felt good on the feet. I told Loren I'd go up the trail and do the same thing, but I wanted at least a little shade.

While sitting with my feet in the stream and my back to the trail, Loren walked past me; neither one saw the other. I waited plenty long for him to put on his shoes and come, but finally I decided to start up the trail. I saw two boys sitting under a ledge in the shade cooling off. I asked if they had seen a boy go up the trail, and they said, "Oh, yes, he was going up the trail and trying to find his dad." They told Loren that a man was up ahead of them. Another man, not me. Two more people gave Loren the same report of a man up ahead of him. They told me the story as we passed. For more than two hours, Loren tried to catch me and I tried to catch him. He had graciously offered to carry the gallon plastic bottle of water, so twice, even though the signs warned it was unsafe, I almost drank out of the stream. When I was most desperate, the people coming down insisted I drink at least a cup of their water.

Indian Gardens is a spring creating this small stream. There was a hydrant below the spring where I started replacing my dehydration. Here I met a woman coming down who said, "Your son is up at the spring and ready to start up the trail again, so you'd better hurry if you want to catch him." Even though I had drunk only five cups of water, I decided to go quickly, and sure enough he was ready to go when we saw each other.

We still had about 5 km (3 miles) up to the South Rim, but now we could relax and choose our speed. However, if we stopped to rest we had to do it standing up. All the rocks were too hot to sit on, even though by now the sun was behind the Canyon wall. We were willing to wait until suppertime for fried ham.

When we arrived at the rim, we had walked 29 km (18 miles) in extreme heat, steep grades down and up, and skirted quite a bit of mule manure and urine-soaked sand. One of the reasons for planning the Canyon trip was to see if we could do it, we had not counted on doing a good part of it alone. We were grateful for the people along the route who helped us reach our goal.

The next day, we went to the Canyon edge for a last look before leaving. Naomi said, "I hear a hummingbird somewhere in a bush," and then I felt the hair on my arms being pulled, and I knew we were being electrostatically charged again. Sure enough, there was another storm in the Canyon, although we had not noticed it until now. We saw the hair standing up on three people's heads. There was no iron railing and we probably were all equally charged, so we experienced no shocks.

We left after we had snapped pictures of people with arms and hair extended, wondering what new challenges could possibly face us on a return visit.

Overcoming All Odds
Gladys O. (DuMond) Zimmerman

Gladys Zimmerman, photo taken during her husband's medical school days.

Born south of Terre Haute, Ind., in 1920, I was fed milk directly from the cow, as my mother was unable to feed me, and Dad knew I was hungry. Dad was a poor preacher, and Mom a disabled schoolteacher. Dad owned a small house in the coal mine district. Unknown to him, the mine dug an illegal tunnel just under the house. No sooner had Dad moved us to Chicago, where he intended to work his way through seminary, when he learned that the house had collapsed in the mineshaft, and all was lost: No recompense or insurance.

Next in the line of troubles, at age 6, I contracted Acute Rheumatic Fever, with severe mitral valve heart damage. My parents were told I would not live beyond my teens, and would certainly die, if I got pregnant. Since penicillin had not yet been invented, and Chicago doctors could do nothing more than tell me to stay as quiet as possible, to protect my heart, my parents took me back to my maternal grandmother, who lived on and operated a farm (Grandpa had a mental disease and had been taken to spend his life in a mental hospital). The good care of my grandmother enabled me to return after a summer, at age 7, to Chicago, where I could look out the dormitory window and watch Jewish kids play in the street. I was not allowed to play, except my Dad taught me to play croquet, and let me beat him just to cheer me up. I read all the books in his library while he worked on the elevated railroad and finished seminary.

After seminary, Dad was assigned to a Home Mission church in eastern Colorado. A severe drought in the 1930s blew away all the topsoil in the area, known in the news as the "dust bowl."

Awakening in the morning, there would be one white spot on my pillow where my head laid; otherwise, a coating of dust. Wells were dry, so water had to be hauled in by tanker and placed in the cistern, which was sanitized by painting it with "whitewash," a lime product.

My little brother was the only one to do the painting, as he was small enough to get through the opening at the top and be let down by ropes. Mom had to strain all of the water to get the centipedes out. Scorpions were a threat: Better knock them out of your shoes before dressing. The only doctor was so busy day and night caring for "dust pneumonia" that he became too drowsy to drive and would call Dad in the middle of the night to drive him for house calls.

Later, we moved to northwest Colorado, to a small town where I worked in the local library after school. A few years in western Kansas, where I graduated from high school, and off I went to Manchester College to major in library science. In my third year, the Lord brought me a husband, who was then in the ministry at $15 per week salary, and doing electric wiring to pay for some graduate school courses at the college. In four months we were married, much to my parents' concern; but my husband was feeling called to Medical Mission work, so off we went to Indiana University Medical School, where I worked in the graduate school and became assistant to the graduate school professor of chemistry. Later, his schooling was moved to the Medical Center in Indianapolis, where I worked as a secretary of Perfection Paint & Color Company, and he worked nights in Catholic hospitals. We together worked his way to a MD without any outside help, though we continued to serve little churches on weekends for a bit more income.

During our time in medical school, I became pregnant (had been told I would die if I did, because of the bad heart valve). However, now we had penicillin. Our first boy was born dead at 7 months, but several years later, while in Detroit doing an internship, we were blessed with a healthy daughter and I didn't die.

We were assigned to China as medical missionaries, and sent to Yale University to study the language, law and customs. At that point, 1947- 48, China was taken over by communists and closed to mission work. We went to the Appalachian coal field, Keokee, Va., and Harlan County, Ky., where our son was born. I taught, English, library, and home economics in the small local school, since no other teacher was available. My husband was the only doctor for miles of mountains, also serving as dentist and veterinarian, there being none of those available. Altogether, we had two years of teaching school, six years in ministry, and 40 years in full medical practice.

Now, he is 91. I, at 87, am disabled by strokes. We find refuge in assisted living. My husband helps me walk as I have no position sense left. Wheelchairs are wonderful.

A.G. Bell
Karen Leigh (Robertson)

A telephone is strong.
    Do you have any idea how much power?
Let me show you.
    A telephone is strong.
But . . . it can't detonate a bomb.
    Now, come along with me.

Your telephone is ringing. You are almost asleep. It's your husband.
His voice is different as he asks, "What are you up to?"
    There is sarcasm when he says, "Wait up for me tonight."
    His voice, really loud now.

Oh, my God! You can't believe what he is saying. His words . . .
like a bomb. Not just any bomb! A Uranus blast you've never felt
before. He repeats himself, "I said, I'm coming home to leave."
    He sensed your disbelief when you didn't respond. He knew he
triggered your deepest fears. He hung up believing you were totally
disconnected now.
    Alexander Graham Bell just allowed a bomb to be dropped, wip-
ing out the electricity in your head.
    You hear his car. Should you wait and watch him come through
the door? Should you greet him?

Suddenly . . . you find yourself rushing toward the key-in-lock
sound remembering the words from your pastor, "You must assure
him that you love him. Assure him that you need him. Make him
understand that you do not want him to leave you."

He's standing in the doorway staring at your tears, and with a
half-cocked grin on his face. You reach out to touch him. He pushes
your touch away. His first words, "I've got to start packing. I'm going
to do you a favor. I'm not taking all of my things tonight. That will
give you time to adjust to the aloneness."

"OH, YEAH!"

All you want is a reason. You want to know WHY! KNOW WHY! KNOW WHY! Almost hysterical, you follow him. First to his dresser. You watch him pick only the newest. You follow him to the closet. You cry! You beg! You don't want him to leave you. You want to know what you are supposed to tell your son. He turns and stares directly into your eyes, "You'll find something to tell him. It would be nice if my leaving could be put in a nice, neat package for you. But it can't!"

He walks out the door. Your eyes are blinded by tears. Your sleep is never the same. Happiness and Mother's Day and anniversaries are never the same. This is how strong Alexander Graham Bell can be.

But Alexander becomes stronger. It's almost midnight. Your telephone is ringing. A drunken voice with slurred words wants to know what you are up to. Still hurting and crying, you do not reply. He curses you. He calls you a slut. He asks if you are sleeping around town. Then . . . he goes for your soft spots and asks, "Who's paying your medical expenses?"

The earth trembled when he blasted you with— "Bitch! You didn't have anything when I married you."

His slurring words pound your ears when he explodes with, "BITCH! I will see you burn in hell!" Remember that one! Burn in hell! Mr. Alexander Graham Bell delivered that gun blast.

What your husband and Mr. Bell didn't know is that your hell had been burning since that midnight when he told you he . . . Do you think Alexander is the type who needs to prove his power or his strength?   Or . . . does just ringing your bell allow him to believe that he has disconnected you?

My Colorful Patchwork Quilt
Rosemary Blosser Fry

When I took early retirement from teaching, I was invited by the quilting women of our congregation to join them in their stitching. I soon became discouraged. My uneven stitches didn't fit with the fine work they were doing.

It occurred to me that while I've been busy doing other things these many years, I have been creating another quilt made of the pieces of my life. Some patches are bright, some dark; some heavy, some light; some smooth, some rough. I have needed to choose, with God's help, how to deal with the squares life has given me.

In the journals I've kept throughout the years I find bits of the fabric of my life. My quilt is unique, but not greatly different from other life quilts. Author Willa Cather says, "There are only two or three human stories and they go on repeating themselves fiercely as if they had never happened before."

Reflecting on my life quilt, I see four main co-designers: my mother, my husband, my children, and my teaching career.

As the youngest, unexpected child in the family, I worried about my mother's health and wondered how I could live without her. Even though I had been an "accident," she never made me feel like a "mistake." I felt treasured by her and my father.

I turned most of the construction over to Paul when we married. Weren't we supposed to become one? Author and teacher David Augsburger says that when two persons try to become one, they have to decide which one. Paul was older and wiser than I, it seemed.

We look for similarities when we choose our mates and then find we are profoundly different. When I realized after a few years that I wasn't sure who I was anymore, I cautiously reached for more of a share in the plan. I found that Paul welcomed it. We are still learning that interdependence is healthy co-dependence.

My children took over my life's design for a time. Having taken a class in childhood psychology in college, I was determined to get an "A" in motherhood. I soon realized that Baby Michael had come with his own degree in management, and it was a toss-up for a while who was in charge. I overheard him saying as a 2-year-old, "Mommy says NO, Mikie says YES." That continued through his adolescence.

One of my brightest birthday squares, however, is the memory of waking up and hearing sounds in the kitchen and going down to find the table set with the best china and crystal. Thirteen-year-old Mike was fixing breakfast as a birthday gift to me.

Brian, born two years after Mike, was an easy-going child, content to be in second place and let Mike be in charge. That changed when he was 5 years old and got to spend three weeks by himself with his grandparents on their farm in Pennsylvania. When he returned home, Mike had a newly independent brother to deal with. Then the fun really began!

The birth of their sister, when the boys were 4 and 6, took some motherly attention and pressure off them as I dealt with Marcia's physical problems. Her short life was a miniature quilt in itself. A new word, "achondroplasia," the medical term for classic dwarfism, became part of my vocabulary soon after her birth. Jagged edges appeared on the quilt pieces of that period of my life. I struggled with the prospect of how life might treat this dark-eyed diminutive daughter who didn't yet know that she was "different."

After Marcia died at age 2 ½, I needed to get out of the house. A new set of blocks was in the making—that of getting back to classroom teaching. Children can tell you that teaching is an easy job. They are the ones who have to do all of the work. One Friday when the principal walked into my classroom to hand me an envelope, a second-grader asked, "What's that?" I told him it was my paycheck. "Oh," he said in surprise, "do you work somewhere?"

Even though I was teaching, I grieved, as I needed to alter and give up the parenting pieces as time went by. I was experiencing what one mother called "an unemployed heart." My children didn't need me anymore.

During the next ten years, four new sparkling quilt blocks warmed me. My grandchildren brought hope and fun with them! The colors of their squares are muted, however, because they live so far away.

Now, I am content to leave the remaining pieces in God's hands. It seems true though, that in many ways "life is what you make of it, and what you make it is up to you."

Fun, Education and Dreams
Kathryn Steckly

Among cornfields and the rolling hills of southeast Iowa in the early 1900s, little one-room schoolhouses where many children received their education dotted the Midwest landscape. My schools, Union and Pacific, provided me with fun, education and dreams.

Kathryn Steckly, front row, second from left, at Union School, Kalona, Iowa, taken approximately 1931.

Getting to school could be a challenge, especially when it rained and I had to negotiate Iowa's sticky mud. When quite small, I got stuck in that awful mud and could go no further. Hearing my lusty wail for help, my mother came to my rescue. A ride on horseback with my dad was very scary. The horse seemed to be a very, very tall one! In winter when the snow was deep, we could walk right over the frozen drifts. Seldom did I get a ride by car. Walking was the expected way of getting to school.

Listening to classes recite provided a rounded education, but I'm sure at times, it was more fun listening to another grade than studying for my next class. When each class met with the teacher, they sat on a bench in front of the room.

People teaching at these rural schools frequently boarded with a family in the school district in order to be closer, as they often didn't have transportation; hence, they walked to school like students. In some cases, teachers were responsible for keeping the fire stoked in the heating system, which sometimes took on the shape of a potbellied stove in the schoolroom. They taught all grades and all subjects. How did they do it all? Teachers also directed Christmas programs for our parents and the community. Getting ready for these occasions was exciting. A lot of time was needed to learn our parts in plays, or a recitation, and the songs we were going to sing. During this time, our studies more or less took the "back seat," which we didn't mind at all! Usually, each student got a bag of candy after the program.

Recess and the noon hour provided times for students to play. When the weather permitted, we played outdoors. Baseball, hide and seek, drop the handkerchief, and other games were our entertainment. The girls enjoyed making houses in a grove of trees. We divided rooms by sweeping dust and pine needles together from one tree to another to form imaginary walls, with an occasional opening for a door.

A wonderful winter activity was sledding. An upperclassman, who was a big guy, would lie on his belly on the sled and two or three of the younger kids would straddle his back. Someone would give us a push and away we went down the hill. As we got older, we would pick up the sled, begin to run, slam the sled to the ground, flop on it on our bellies, and go flying down the hill. Wheeee!

Our small library included a set of well-used encyclopedia, "The Book of Knowledge." Here in this one-room school I began to dream. In geography, my favorite subject, I'd read about the world and many far-off places, The Seven Wonders of the Modern World, The Seven Wonders of the Ancient World, and more. I dreamed of one day visiting some far-off places. What an imagination for a young girl who had never met a world traveler.

How I wanted to see the Matterhorn in Switzerland, Victoria Falls in Africa, the pyramids and sphinx in Egypt, and more. Those long time dreams were eventually fulfilled when I traveled to Europe and later served with a travel agency in East Africa.

Experiencing the snowy peak of the Matterhorn piercing the blue sky from a little village bed and breakfast at its foot was a fulfilled dream. Seeing the majestic Victoria Falls and hearing the roar of the falling water was an awesome thrill. Climbing through a pyramid in a stooped position following the guide who kept saying, "Slowly, slowly," provided a challenge. Completing the desert experience was a ride on the back of "the ship of the desert."

These three encounters, and many more, filled my life with beauty, awe, and an awareness of the wide, wide world in which I live.

Nearly eight decades ago, the dreams of that little girl linger in my memory and I still find myself dreaming of seeing more of this world, which will now be dreams from my chair. All of this has been a wonderful gift from the education that I received in that one-room school in southeast Iowa. Thank you, Union and Pacific, for the fun, education and dreams.

Glimpses of a Country School – 1952-53
Ruth Conrad Liechty

As I drove along the gravel and dirt roads to Douglas School three miles southwest of Wayland in southeastern Iowa, I tried to ignore thoughts of the dream that had recurred repeatedly during the past several nights. I was totally unfamiliar with one-teacher country schools (grades 1-8).

Since I attended the same congregation as many of the Douglas students, I had been hearing rumors about the school. Last year's teacher had "let the students do as they pleased." Some days he had simply not appeared, and after waiting and waiting, the children had returned home. He had told them that they did not need to learn the multiplication tables, yet most of them received straight A's on their report cards.

Douglas School, Henry County, Iowa. Sketch by Ruth Liechty.

In my dream, this first day had been chaos. Instead of coming to their seats when I rang the bell, they had to be corralled on the play-ground. When a few of them were in their seats, I'd go out after the others and the first would run outdoors.

I expected to arrive at the schoolhouse at least half an hour before any of the students. To my chagrin, students were waiting for me. Not only were they waiting, they followed me into the school-house, put their lunch pails on the shelf in the cloakroom, came into the classroom and took seats. Instead of needing to corral them, I wondered how to get them outside so I could collect my thoughts and do final preparations for the day. But, they sat—and smiled at me.

Finally, I decided that since they were all present and seated, I might as well ring the bell and begin the school day early lest they wander out and my dream still come true. As I did, the president of the school board walked in, amazed to find the school day already beginning.

I had no idea how to organize the day except to schedule a 15-minute morning and afternoon recess and one-hour lunch/recess break at noon. But, with the 46 textbooks for the seven classes (19 students, but none in seventh grade that year, sigh!), how was I to organize the remainder of the day? Besides the opening, my schedule was divided into five-minute class periods—enough time to collect the previous day's work, provide a bit of review/discussion, and explain the next assignment. Fortunately, this was the first year the country schools were exempted from having kindergarten. At least my first-graders could already do some reading. Imagine the amount of work facing me at the end of the school day. I had a typewriter and a gelatin mimeograph "pan."

Four weeks later the superintendent for the country schools held a teachers' meeting. What an eye opener! At least I had some idea about what questions to ask and I did a lot of listening. I also went home wishing I would not need to face anyone at church on Sunday. No such option. Parents and relatives commented about what positive reports they had heard of me. I wished I could drop into a hole and disappear.

Monday morning I announced a new schedule and procedures to the children. A sign of relief went over the room. Moreover, while I had learned to get to school earlier, the students were learning to appreciate recesses and how to organize themselves to play games while I stayed indoors.

One cold winter Sunday afternoon my father went to the schoolhouse to restart the coal furnace in the basement. He expertly banked the fire. Thus, Monday morning there were hot coals ready to get the fire blazing. However, firing the furnace was another skill I needed to learn. Finally, the three eighth-grade girls (no boys in that class) begged to be allowed to go fire up the furnace. The schoolroom soon became warm—and warmer. I went to the basement. The girls had opened the draft—and left it open. Flames were roaring and the furnace glowed red. I feared a fire and quickly closed the draft.

The schoolhouse did not burn down—nor did I ever again let students take charge of the furnace.

Spring thaws and rains came. I could not take the short route, for half of the four miles were sticky with Iowa mud. At least the seven-mile route was all gravel. One rainy morning when I was nearly at the schoolhouse, I realized I had left the school key at home. In desperation, I stopped at the home of one of my students and asked to use the phone. I called home to ask if my father could bring the key. The student's mother overheard the conversation. She suggested that I call the school board president and ask him to unlock the door, since he would probably be bringing the children to school anyway. Even more embarrassed, I agreed to do so. As I picked up the receiver to place the call, I became newly aware that this was a party line. I overheard one parent offering to pick up another parent's children, but adding, "I guess we don't have to be in a hurry. The teacher forgot her key."

Still, near the end of the school year, I was asked to return. By the beginning of the fourth year, toilets with heat lamps had even been installed in the basement.

Miss Conlin's 'Treat'
Bobbie Lee Hudson

We were sixth graders in Miss Conlin's class. Faithfully, during our lunch period, we would march over to the tiny mom and pop grocery store located across the street. There we would spend a penny or two, buying our favorite candy treat. In those days, a penny or two provided a fist full of treats.

Our dilemma was our teacher's continuous request for one of our treats. She would walk into the classroom and spot our stash. Then she'd say, "May I try one?" What could we say?

So . . . one day, out of sheer desperation, we huddled together just before her grand entrance. A FIREBALL would be her "treat."

Sure enough, came time for the honored request. A designated student (I still remember his name) who was seated up front, quietly handed her the cellophane wrapped "treat."

We sat there, not even daring to breathe, God forbid, or look at each other. Miss Conlin reverently sucked on our "treat." In less than a minute, she quietly and quickly retreated to her closet. This is where she kept a small spray bottle that she used to spray her mouth.

When she emerged from the closet, she was quite composed and confident. Needless to say, Miss Conlin never, ever again asked us for one of our precious, delicious, lunchtime treats.

My Nursing Experiences
M. J. Richardson, R.N.

My earliest desire was to be a kindergarten teacher, but with the depression years, I knew I could not enter this field. My next choice was nursing. Our family doctor had performed an appendectomy on me, and I had discussed in length my desire to enter the nursing field. Along with my family, he encouraged me. He was impressed with Indiana University School of Nursing and wanted me to apply for entrance.

After graduation from high school in June of 1933, I started working as a clerk in the cutting department of Wilson Brothers Shirt Factory making a fabulous salary of $15 per week. I had worked my way up to $18 before resigning and going to school.

I applied for admission to Indiana University in winter of 1934 and was accepted for the class of February 1935. I was required to travel to Indianapolis to school prior to my acceptance for a physical and a personal interview by the director, Miss Cordelia Hoeflin. I had anticipated this to be a really traumatic experience, but she was a lovely person and I was immediately at ease.

A few weeks after this experience, I was rewarded with a letter of acceptance. It was necessary to assemble articles of clothing, order uniforms and shoes, and get all needed articles organized for school.

The day came for me to depart and my mother and brother drove me from South Bend to Indianapolis and my assigned room at 3rd Cottage on the medical center campus. We were assigned roommates. I drew a gal from Illinois who was short and appeared studious. My mother was so impressed because she had placed a Bible on her desk. She didn't last long because she was a wild little gal, who would sneak in and out of windows for late dates. She was a good student and book learning came easy for her. She apparently came from a nice family who was strict, but she really went wild. The school would not tolerate her constant breaking of the rules, and so that was the end of my first roommate.

There were many experiences during my first year. I worked on a ward for postoperative gynecological surgical patients. It was a great place to get lots of experience. The head nurse had a great reputation for being very exacting and hypercritical. She was a taskmaster, but an excellent teacher and a lovely person.

Money was scarce during those post Depression days. My parents sent me one dollar week. It was amazing the things I could do with that dollar. Almost everyone was on a limited allowance, so I was definitely not deprived. Miss Hoeflin, the director of nurses, wanted us to enjoy ourselves, but being a lady was a definite requirement. One always had a current love, and life was full of fun along with classes and studying and really hard work on the wards of the Indiana University Hospitals.

The sessions of letting off steam after hours on duty were many and of long duration. The context of these sessions are vague, but certainly we gained knowledge and perhaps at times some true facts were blown way out of proportion by the teller of the tale.

The morning prayer after breakfast left a lasting impression. Miss Hoeflin would read a short scripture from the Bible and we would all sing a hymn. Sometimes, Miss Hoeflin would call students out of line for a short conference or a reprimand for a flaw in personal appearance.

After receiving my graduate nurse pin, I went home for a few days of vacation and returned to start duty as a scrub nurse at Robert Long Hospital. It wasn't long before I was being trained to scrub for neurosurgeons. Some seemed to be a little irritable and terribly spoiled by the lesser doctors and nurses because of their abilities. I learned to enjoy surgery sessions and realized they were only human and not God.

So many successful surgeries to save lives, improve birth defects, both orthopedics and plastic types, were done daily at Riley's Hospital. All this we give credit to our dear Lord who made possible all these wonderful accomplishments in our lives.

My Good Friend, Mitcha Froy
Naomi Waggy

During the Great Depression my home was in the capital city of Harrisburg, Pa. I was the second oldest in a closely-knit family with five girls and a baby boy, Theodore.

In our community we helped each other so no one would go hungry. Mother spent many hours sewing clothes for others. She was missionary-minded and regularly went with my dad to assist in pastoral calling.

On one visitation, my parents met a lady named Mrs. Schroy. She lived just a few blocks from the parsonage, with her ill and unemployed husband and sons, George (18), and Charles (16). George was shy and spent much time at home. Charles, too, was very dependent on his mother.

Mrs. Schroy became our faithful "babysitter." From the beginning she tried hard to do her work well and be friendly to our whole family. Each day she prepared food on our big black cookstove for our family of eight, and also to have enough to take home for her family of four.

We liked her and lovingly called her "Mitcha Froy." Many afternoons we used a large pan, or big bowls and bags to carry the food to her home. It sometimes seemed like a long walk. From that experience, at the age of 7, I was praised for being her good helper.

During the day, Charles often came to our kitchen door to ask his mother for a nickel for ice cream, or just anything as an excuse to see her. He might interrupt our noon meal with an excuse to see her because he had stubbed his toe, or had bitten his tongue, or he couldn't find a clean shirt. Several times I heard my mother remark that "someday Charles will grow up and think for himself."

It seemed to me our brother Theodore got more attention from Mitcha Froy than the rest of us. We were often reminded that because he was a boy, we were fortunate to be blessed with a brother. Therefore, any bit of his immaturity was to be tolerated. I began to learn the meaning of the phrase, "being spoiled." We loved him, anyway, because he was our little, cute baby brother.

My father liked to tell friends, "I am the father of five daughters and each one has a brother." I remember being in the room with my sisters while Dad phoned many friends to announce the birth of his son. The name Theodore Emmanuel means "gift of God with us."

Each school morning, Mitcha Froy would comb and braid the long hair of each girl. Often she would speak in her own Pennsylvania Dutch language, "Dradich hroom, consign ee gunsadoom!" Translated, that meant"Turn around and don't be so dumb." She was fun!

Somehow my mother had a special way of sharing her love with each one of her children. She was a positive thinker. She sang many different hymns as she worked at doing laundry, cleaning, or other jobs. Often we sang together as we washed the dishes. On Saturdays, Mother always baked several pies for Sunday dinner that followed the church service. We never knew who'd be invited to eat with us.

Mother's singing was good therapy for all of us. When I asked Mitcha Froy if she liked to hear Mother sing so much, she replied, "Sure, I do!" I liked for Mitcha Froy to rock me in the big oak rocker. I curled up in her lap and she would rock and rock and sing and sing. One of her favorite song texts was "Let the merry sunshine in. Let the merry sunshine in! Open all the windows. Open all the doors. Let the merry sunshine in!" However, never did she sing the same note on the same word. I tried to think of a nice way to tell her how much I wished that when we sang her song together she should always sing the same tune. Nevertheless, I believe Mitcha Froy's way of singing helped me decide that my life's mission would be to teach people how to sing and enjoy music.

Later I graduated from college as a music major and found opportunities to teach many thousands of children to enjoy singing. I immensely enjoyed teaching elementary music in the Goshen Schools for 18 years. A child singing in a monotone voice was a pleasant challenge for me because I found it to be a strong unbroken thread of love shining from my acquaintance with Mitcha Froy.

Now, as I see an entry I wrote in a "baby book" for one of my sons, I am puzzled. The writing shows that when he was 5 years old he prayed this daily prayer: "Dear God. Be nice and good. Let babysitters go to OTHER people's houses. All things we have! Amen." How I wish he could have had a babysitter like my good friend, Mitcha Froy!

Let There Be Light
Patricia Whyte McKinney

"Always be a helper, always be a helper, Patricia," my Grandfather Heise softly said to me over and over again as he blew smoke rings into my ears when I was 4 years old and suffering severe earaches. They only went away when I had a tonsillectomy at age 5. George Washington Heise had 12 children and my mother, Mabel Heise Whyte, was the oldest of the three daughters. After Grandmother Heise died when I was 2 years old, Grandfather visited us for about a month at a time and, oh, how it relieved those earaches I was experiencing.

About once a week, Grandfather would walk up to Main Street for a shave and a haircut, and us three grandchildren would be delighted when he returned with boxes of Cracker Jacks for us. Mary Shaw Heise had been one of 21 children born to an early physician. He had three wives and as each one died he married again and had more children.

On my dad's side of the family, my great-grandfather and his brothers were in a one-room schoolhouse in Denny, Scotland. The teacher said, "W-H-I-T-E is such a common word; why don't you change your name to Whyte?" And so they did. My great-grandfather's family in Scotland were weavers of paisley. Marco Polo brought paisley designs from the Far East.

Great-grandfather Ebenezer Whyte married Sophia Pritchard, daughter of the astronomer for Queen Victoria. They had four children and at first lived in Chicago. Then, Ebenezer took a train to Kansas City, Mo. His seat mate was William Rockhill Nelson.

In Kansas City, Ebenezer Whyte opened the Whyte Grain and Wine Company, which he eventually named the Whyco Stores. My parents met in France in World War I. My dad was proud of the fact he never carried a gun . . . the fact was, his footlocker was lost on the ship going overseas. He was an officer in the Quartermasters Corps and my mother was a registered nurse, also an officer. They met at a dance for officers. They were engaged to be married for a year. My dad stayed overseas putting things away. Mom later told me he was doing the work of two men at the time. She traveled to Alsace

Lorraine and other places of interest in France before returning to the United States.

They lived with my Great-grandfather and Great-grandmother Whyte in a large comfortable house located in The Country Club Plaza district of Kansas City. When my sister was born July 11, 1921, they washed out her diapers in the bathtub. That address was 12 East Concord. Ebenezer Whyte had purchased The Waverly Block in north Kansas City where the others built large apartments where they lived.

When I arrived on April 11, 1923, my parents moved four blocks to 5139 Baltimore, which my grandparents gave them the land and the house. Across the street was Visitation Catholic School and there were many playthings on the playground we could use when school was out.

In first grade at E.C. White School where we attended, I remember being very shy, not speaking up much. Also, I was not learning to read, just sitting at my desk staring out the window. Then one afternoon I was playing outside and my first-grade teacher, Miss Higman, came up the walk and knocked at our front door. Every night after, my mother read to Mary, my sister and me. We shared a bed. I found out what reading meant. The Bobbsey Twins books, Heidi, Winnie the Pooh, The Nancy Drew mysteries, and on and on.

When I was in fourth grade at E.C. White, my teacher, Miss Dorothy Matthews, asked the class, "Is there anyone who made you feel welcome when you came here?" The little girl sitting near me raised her hand and gave my name. Sarah played the violin and often performed at P.T.A. meetings. The last I heard of Sarah Caldwell, she was pictured on Time magazine as the director of the Opera Company of Boston.

We graduated in seventh grade to go on to high school. Miss Edna Green was my seventh-grade teacher and Miss Inez Black, our school principal. For the graduation service each of the 25 other students said a short paragraph, after which my assigned line was "Let there be light."

Now I am 84 years old. One morning I awoke with this song: "Jesus is my light. Jesus is my light. Jesus is the light of my life."

My Journey
Lena Poindexter

I was born a sharecropper's daughter in a small town, Grays, Arkansas, December 22, 1928. I was the third of four girls. We were very poor, and started working in the cotton field at a very early age. Even though we were poor, I was happy.

God had blessed me with spiritual gifts. I started singing, and speaking in churches at the age of 6. My parents gave me the best education they could afford. Opportunities were not that great where were lived. I graduated from 12th grade in 1949.

We moved to South Bend, Ind., in 1950 looking for a better life. The first thing I did was go looking for a job. Jobs weren't that easy to find. I didn't understand why because I was a good person and a hard worker.

The second thing I did was find a church home. I joined the Mount Olive Baptist Church, where I sang in the choir and spoke on several programs. After hearing me speak and emcee several programs, I was given the name, "The Little Lady with the Golden Voice." The famous gospel singers would get me to emcee their big programs. I traveled from city to city.

The Lord blessed me with two beautiful daughters. My oldest went home to be with the Lord on May 30, 1969 at the tender age of 19. It left such a void in my life, but she also left me with a healthy grandson. He was only 5 months old. With the Lord's help, I raised him to be a great young man. He graduated head of his class, went to college and earned B.A. and Master's degrees. He never gave me a minute's trouble. He is now married with two beautiful girls and another on the way. He has a lovely wife, beautiful home, and good job. My other daughter has two sons, beautiful home, and good job. Her oldest son has a good job and her youngest son is a senior in college.

In 1987, I became a member of a bus fellowship group that goes on tour twice a year, in May and October. It was organized so poor people could get to go places and see things at a very low price. We go to a different state each trip. The trip is for five days. Wherever we go, I'm scheduled to speak that Sunday morning for church. I have been to many beautiful places and met lots of nice people. The Lord has been good to me.

I am now 79 years old, living in a senior apartment building, in good health, still working at Cardinal Rehab. I have been there for 23 years.

I am very active in my church and community. I keep busy speaking at different churches for anniversaries, men's and women's day celebrations, funerals, and so on. I am often asked if I'm a teacher, preacher or writer. My answer is that I am just a servant.

I always encourage the women at my church to stay busy. There is plenty for us to do to help our young ladies. We do not need to compete with men, that is not our purpose here. We were not created to be a second-rate man, but mother of mankind, loving and kind. We should set good examples for our young people.

I pray to God each day to continue to use me in His service. When the Lord tells me, well done, it will not mean I was cremated, but I always did my best.

My Irish Great-Grandmother Jemima
Wilma Edith Hollopeter Shank

Knowing the Swiss Mennonite and German Brethren backgrounds of my parents, Velma Spicher and Ray Hollopeter, I was to learn with great delight in recent years that I also have Irish roots in the person of my great-grandmother, Jemima Gardner.

Jemima's father, James Gardner, came to America in the late 1770s when Irish tenant farmers were living in extreme poverty. Said to "have come from Baptist folks," he made the long voyage from Ireland to America when he was a lad of about 16 years of age. James was invited to live with a relative in Princeton, N.J., and had been promised help with his future education.

As a new "patriot," James joined the Continental Army in Princeton in 1777 when British and Continental troops under General Washington were fighting over the town; he then served under Washington until the end of the war. He was with General George Washington in the conclusive battle of Yorktown in October 1781. There, he reportedly performed an act of valor and a personal favor for Washington, for which he was personally remembered and thanked by the Commander-in-Chief. At some point, he received the honorary title of "Colonel." Although he never commanded troops, for the rest of his life he was proudly known as "Colonel Gardner."

When the war was over, James learned the trade of a tailor as an apprentice, and worked in a tailor shop in Philadelphia, then the national capital. He later "boasted" that he had tailored a suit of clothes for President Washington (ca. 1791). Indeed, Colonel Gardner's eldest daughter, Margaretta, later known popularly as "Aunt Marg'et," remembered hearing her father tell of his meeting General Washington in a room at the Masonic Lodge, where she thought they were both members. She recalled her father telling of participating in a game of nine pins with Washington; George was reportedly a player second to none.

Gardner's frugality permitted him later to purchase the shop in which he had been an apprentice. After a fire destroyed his Philadelphia house and business, including an unpaid stock of cloth, he was bankrupt. He was said to have gotten "Western Fever" and went to the western frontier in West Moreland County, east of Pittsburgh in the 1790s. He later moved northeast to the small, emerging Pennsylvania town of Indiana, the county seat of Indiana County.

In Indiana, Gardner set up a tailor shop; business was very poor since everyone wore homemade clothing. Here were only a few houses in the town. The place was overgrown with "blackjack and scrub white oaks." It was in the town of Indiana that Colonel Gardner met and married Mary Coulter, the daughter of the second settler of the town, William Coulter, probably of Scots origin. Jemima was reportedly their fifth child, but her date of birth is unknown.

Gardner soon bought some 40 acres of land in Center Township at $5 an acre. He is listed on the tax roll of 1807. In 1820, when he was about 60 years of age, after having been crippled by being thrown from a horse, he built a log house there "in the wilds" for himself and his family. So, my Great-grandmother Jemima, in her teenage years, grew up in a frontier log cabin in the forest of western Pennsylvania. In time, she married Daniel Spicher, from Swiss Anabaptist immigrants, who had also settled in Indiana County where there were apparently no other Mennonites. Jemima and Daniel were both a part of a local Baptist congregation, and lived near Hillsdale (Indiana County) where he was a farmer, a woodsman, and a person of considerable influence.

Jemima's son, my grandfather William Gardner Spicher, was born in 1856, apparently the third of six children. During the Civil War, Daniel volunteered as an infantryman and served until the end of the war with other Union recruits from Pennsylvania. While his father was gone to war, my Grandfather William recalls how he plowed and cultivated with horses at the age of 8. Jemima was still living at the time of Daniel's return from the war in early 1864, but died after the birth of their fifth child, before 1867.

One can recognize the very deep attachment Jemima had to her Irish family roots by choosing to give her son William the middle name of "Gardner." William Gardner Spicher was my maternal grandfather. He joined the Mennonite Church when he was already an adult and was later ordained as a deacon. He was called "Pap" by his own children, following the popular Irish usage of his mother

Jemima, in reference to her own husband and William's father, Daniel Spicher. After Jemima's death, he later remarried and with Rebecca O'Harra had five more children, the first of which was born in February 1868.

This brief article reminds me that at that time, much more was written about the lives and happenings of men than about women. Yet, we do possess a photograph of my Great-grandmother Jemima as a young woman. Her hair is pulled back rather severely, as was so often the custom, and around her neck she is wearing a string of equally-sized round beads. A maternal aunt reported that at that time such beads were said to be worn for protection against influenza.

I was indeed surprised and very happy to discover that I have an important streak of Irish blood in my veins. My husband now understands better from whence comes what he calls my "special spunk and spark."

My Grandparents' Pre-Arranged Marriage
Carol Bogol

Both of my grandparents were born in 1881, one day apart. My grandmother was born in Poland and came to the United States with her parents before she was one year old. My grandmother's three brothers and four sisters were all born in the United States in the State of Pennsylvania.

My grandfather was born in Prague, Czechoslovakia, and came to the United States at the age of 19 in 1900 with his younger brother, and settled in Pennsylvania. They left behind their parents and five siblings. In three years, their mother and four siblings would be joining them (their father had died and was buried in Prague). My grandfather's older sister did not wish to leave the country.

My grandmother was introduced to her future husband in the parlor of her home. Her parents and my grandfather's mother knew each other and they planned and arranged the marriage prior to the meeting of my grandparents. My grandmother was very hurt because she was in love with the butcher who worked at the corner grocery store. However, she could not go against her parents' wishes, so she consented to the marriage even though her heart was broken. She and my grandfather were married in Blossburg in 1903.

My grandfather was a carpenter by trade and supported his new wife by working in the coal mines. Their first daughter was born in 1904 and they had heard work was opening up in South Bend. They packed their belongings along with their daughter and came to South Bend to look for work. My grandfather found just what he was qualified to do and that was with the Singer Factory making cabinets for the sewing machines. They purchased a home near their Polish church and lived there for their entire lives.

They added to their family by having six more girls. They had four boys who all died in infancy. My grandmother's family came from Pennsylvania and lived in South Bend a few blocks away from my grandparents' house, helping to care for the seven girls. My grandfather's family continued to live in Pennsylvania. In 1956 and 1957, my grandparents died one year and one day apart. Even though their marriage was preplanned, it was successful and there was much love in my family.

The Day I Met My Grandmother
Lora Miranda

The day finally came when my grandma, a missionary in India, returned to stay. I was going to meet her for the first time. Don't ask me the day of the week or the month of the year. I only know that I was 7, so, it must have been 1944.

It was summer. I remember standing around outside without coats or jackets on the day she arrived. She traveled from India in a ship, probably landing in New York. I think she came to Chicago by train. Someone received her there and brought her by car to our house in Elkhart, Ind.

As we awaited her arrival, it seemed my father thought it was taking far too long. Grandma should be there by now. He was impatient, not having seen his mother for quite a few years. Not many cars came down our short street on an afternoon. Dad paced around the front yard peering down the street to see if any cars were turning, it would surely be she if there were. I entertained myself by watching Dad. The excitement was almost too much! Finally, a car did come and Dad shouted, "Here they come!" We all rushed out to the front yard.

Suddenly, a tall, stout woman flew into my father's arms and he began to cry. Grandma was saying over and over, "My, son, my son!" Not many times had I ever seen my father cry. After a time, my mother, sister, little brother and I got our hugs as well. When my turn came, I felt I was extra special. She wasn't beautiful, but she was absolutely wonderful and just as grandmotherly as I thought a grandmother should be.

Then a tall, gangly teenaged girl got out of the car and stood beside her. It was my youngest aunt, Clara. She was the only one of my aunts I didn't know. She laughed a lot and we soon got acquainted. After much chatter, the luggage was unloaded. It included numerous big brown suitcases and leather-strapped, humped trunks that looked just fascinating. I suppose later we had a meal together.

I don't remember what we ate or what else occurred, because I only watched my Grandma's every move and followed her everywhere, just like a puppy. I was in awe. This lady had lived in India and could speak Hindi! She traveled on ships and trains and she had all those intriguing looking pieces of luggage!

When some of those trunks were opened, they contained treasures. Two girl-sized "saris" for my sister and I were there. Grandma showed us how to wear them. There were ivory carved elephants and a beautiful Blue Willow pattern china tea set for our doll parties, which she had purchased in Calcutta.

I don't remember how long she and Aunt Clara stayed with us. We had a rather small house and she had to sleep in the same bedroom with my sister and me. I was awed again and thought surely she had come straight down from heaven when I saw her reading from a well-worn Bible. Then she knelt by the bed and prayed. To me it seemed at least like an hour.

Grandma Esch did become our nanny for a few weeks when my younger sister was born. Although she did not make her home in Indiana, our family did go over many rivers and down many highways to visit her in Illinois, Colorado, and finally Showalter Villa in Hesston, Kan. She made delicious Indian food as well as other more traditional dishes. I ate rivel soup for the first time in my life at her table. I have many happy memories of playing games, singing in Hindi, listening to her stories, and just enjoying her presence for many years.

Although sometimes after the day we first met I thought she was rather stern and strict, her love was always felt. The influence of her constant prayers for all of us can never be measured. I believe she influenced me for voluntary service in the church and the decision to go to another country. She lived to be 96 and kept a very clear and sharp mind. She always wanted to know what was going on in each of her grandchildren's busy lives.

I'm glad I met my grandmother one happy day when I was 7. Her name was Mina Brubaker Esch.

The Big Fish
Laverne Nafziger

My parents, Milton and Esther Vogt, were missionaries in India assigned to the station in Ghatula for the first six years of service. In 1934, they were moved to Balodgahan for a year while Daddy served as mayor, or "mulgazar" of the Christian village located at that mission station. Here, we were much closer to many of the other mission families.

Our family lived in a large bungalow. One of the features that made the buildings cooler were the wide verandas, or porches, on several sides of the building. These were wonderful places for us children, Merle, 5, and me, 3 years old, to play. There was plenty of room for running and riding tricycles.

One day I was running up and down the five steps of the veranda. When I was at the top step, I was trying to jump across the corner where the steps joined the veranda. Looking down into the space

where the steps joined the veranda I saw a "big fish." I ran quickly to Daddy's office. Excitedly I told him, "Daddy, there is a big fish out there."

Knowing that we were a long way from water, Daddy went with me to check out this "big fish." When he saw what was curled up in the corner of the steps and the veranda, he quickly got his gun.

The other missionaries came over to celebrate the outcome of this adventure. In the Gospel Herald printed for May 17, 1934, there was a photo of Ralph Smucker standing on a box, one arm reaching up as far as he could, holding the tail end of a python. The caption under the picture reads:

A Snake, 7 ft. 10 inches long, shot beside the Balodgahan Bungalow. The snake was first seen by Laverne Vogt, 3 years old. Brother Smucker is seen holding the Snake.

The Bus Ride
Bertha Beachy

I walked toward the waiting bus with students and fellow teachers. Classes finished at 1:00 p.m. and all of us wanted to return the 15 miles to Mogadishu, the capital city of Somalia. I noticed the signs sprouting everywhere on campus, SOUTH VIETNAM HAS FALLEN. WE SUPPORT THE FORCES OF NORTH VIETNAM. I suddenly realized that I represented the enemy on campus because of my nationality.

I had just come from teaching a class of 35 Islamic teachers who taught in the Qur'anic schools across Somalia. They spoke Arabic fluently but they wanted to learn English. They loved having a native English speaker as their teacher. They were wonderful students and treated me with great respect. They also came to Lafoole, the name of this teacher training school, from all over Somalia.

The more than 50 some teachers came from Somalia, Egypt, Pakistan and East Germany. I was the lone American, Christian and woman among the teachers. We shared a common teachers' lounge. With more than 16 years of living and working in Somalia, I loved it. A military coup followed the burial of the assassinated Somali president on Oct. 21,1969. The new government turned to the east and embraced Scientific Socialism. Most Americans left soon after this, including those who had begun Lafoole.

Three years later, they announced the writing of the Somali language. They nationalized all private schools, which included the mission schools. Though the mother tongue was Somali, Somalis had studied in four foreign languages. At that point we offered the mission teachers to the Ministry of Education. They placed 10 of us in government schools. I had started teaching in a third secondary school when the Minister of Education asked me to transfer to Lafoole. At this point, I was into my second year of teaching at Lafoole.

I boarded the bus and went to the back since I got off at the last stop. I noticed that Musa, the foremost Somali poet living inside Somalia, joined us on the bus. He nodded to me as he sat down. Earlier, I had sold some of his books in the mission bookstore that I had managed. Someone asked him to recite Somali poetry. Poets are held in the highest esteem as they aptly honor Somali culture. Musa went to the front of the bus and stood facing all of us. He supported himself by standing with his back against a pole.

He recited stanza after stanza of his unwritten poetry. All of us listened with rapt attention as he recited in classical Somali about the life of the traditional Somali camel herder contrasted with life in the city. He touched many Somali cultural and religious issues, but nothing about the coup. I was startled when he stopped abruptly. He had used the word, "infidel." He announced in English for all of us to hear, "That's not you, Miss Beachy; you believe in God!"

I sat very quietly as Musa continued. It seemed important to not be noticed. I realized that Musa valued my faith as I valued his.

Hair Pin Repair in the Serengeti
Miriam Charles

Our one year of service in Ghana, West Africa, would end soon. We, Howard, Thomas and I, made plans for the return home to Goshen, Ind. I was eager to return by the shortest route possible. I thought we would just reverse the route flown in 1973. But Howard had another idea, which was to return by way of East Africa to visit Mennonite missions there. He knew the first, and some the present, missionaries. Now was the opportunity to see the fruit of their labors. Thomas, our 13-year-old interested in flying and liking it, favored the longest route home. Overcoming my reluctance, I also accepted it.

The missionaries at Shirati encouraged us to make a one-day and overnight excursion to the Serengeti National Park to see the exotic animals in their native habitat. Thomas and Howard readily agreed, and I was dragging my feet. No more delays for me—I wished to go home. After one of the missionaries offered his Peugeot to make the trip, I weakened and agreed to go, again overcoming my reluctance.

As I remember, we were given oral instructions but no printed ones. There was no superhighway, but a narrow dirt "path" to follow. And since we were in the dry season, rain should not cause problems. This information given sincerely came back to haunt us in the hours ahead.

Our first test for remembering the oral instructions given us came when reaching a fork in the road. Should we turn left or right? We chose left. Continuing on our way, we soon saw a car stopped on the narrow road ahead. Immediately we stopped, with no space to pass or pull alongside the other car. The driver got out and came to talk with us. We learned that he, his wife, and a German friend were out to see the wonders in the park just as we were. Something in the motor had broken and now they were stranded in bush country without access to repair service. He asked if we might have some wire with us; he thought he could make the repair if only he had wire. We searched the borrowed car but found no wire. What could be done where we had this "in the middle of nowhere" feeling?

A light came on for me, the one reluctant to make this excursion! There were wire hair pins in my hair holding it in place! I pulled out one of the two-and-one-half inch pieces of wire, showed it to the doctor, we had learned he was an M.D. serving in Tanzania, and demonstrated it could easily be bent into five inches of useable wire. He looked, took it, and returned to work on his car.

Eureka! The motor hummed to life, and the grateful doctor returned to offer profuse thanks. He wondered about our travel plans and on learning we planned to continue on further into the Serengeti suggested we might wish to stay within sight of one another. Did he think I had more wire to give? We had already gone only a short distance, yet far enough to realize there would be security in having traveling companions. We agreed to stay within sight of one another and this was proven to be a good decision.

The information given to us about this time of year being the dry season had been correct. No rain fell while we were traveling, but it had previous to the dry season with the result still in evidence. The small rivulets crossing our road had swelled into swollen streams covering the road crossing with water of an unknown depth. There was no choice; forward into the water was the way to go. The doctor and Howard, who was driving our car, rolled up their pant legs, got out of the cars into the water, and pushed. This activity was repeated a number of times until natives began appearing out of the bush on either side of the road, offering their service. There were two grateful men ready to accept this. The doctor rewarded them with cigarettes. This happened often enough that the doctor thought his supply might be exhausted before reaching our destination. It was a mystery to us how natives appeared at the right time to help when we had not seen them until we were in the water. We thought there was some kind of secret communication going on from one crossing to the next.

Eventually we reached the lodge where our traveling companions had reservations for the night, and we did not. Fortunately for us, there was a room for us, too!

In addition to the other experiences we had was the wonder of viewing elephants, giraffes, lions, wildebeests and other animals in their natural setting. Even if at times I felt as if we were at the end of the world and home in Goshen far away, we returned. Now, 33 years later, I am writing about it—a vivid memory.

The Hail Storm
Jan Hughey

There was a time I drove quite a distance three times a week to see a chiropractor who also specialized in acupressure (not acupuncture). I got a lot of relief by him working on pressure points; he also taught me to lie on tennis balls at home on these spots to relieve spasms and pain. It was worth the drive.

A friend or relative often accompanied me, but one sunny day I was alone. The doctor wanted me to be active, so on the way home I would stop at a supermarket to walk the aisles; the store also doubled 75 cent coupons, so I could save at the same time. As the bagger put the items in the car, I casually mentioned, "It looks like it's going to rain."

By the time I got to the street from the parking lot, the rain had started. I pulled into traffic behind a semi and another semi pulled behind me; I was the meat in a truck sandwich. The rain poured! A short distance later, the rain turned to hail. It covered the windshield so much that I could not see out--it was as though the windshield was painted white. The noise was horrendous! I prayed, no, yelled, "PLEASE DON'T LET MY WINDOWS BREAK!" I imagined a lap full of glass and ice. We are taught to be specific when we pray, so I named what I needed: my windows to remain intact.

There was another dilemma: I had not hit the semi in front of me; that meant he had not stopped. Was the one behind me still rolling, too? I supposed they were in CB radio communication with each other to know what they were doing. I crept along to lessen the impact of the impending crash. None occurred.

Having no companion with me that day was a blessing–imagine her fears while I would make frustrating decisions. Hours later, well, a few minutes anyway–if not long seconds–the sky cleared. I saw a set of tire tracks in the oncoming lane beside me on the highway. Unknowingly, a vehicle had passed in the opposite direction, but I was the only one on the road! No truck or other car was around. It seemed eerie. I saw a pull-off spot and stopped, shook, praised the Lord and cried. I learned later a tornado had gone through a nearby town and the hail was part of that weather system.

We called the car "Dimples" after that. Here were pock marks all over it, including the bright work, but no window was chipped!

When I returned the next time, I saw the road through different eyes. Each side has an eight-foot drainage ditch; if a power steering wheel turns ever so slightly, the whole car goes off the road. When I was blinded by the hail and saw the tire tracks beside me, I now knew I had stayed straight without head-on impact. I could have even gone into one of the ditches. I also knew I had not traveled alone that day–I had an Unseen Companion. WHAT A BLESSING!

I have a ceramic basket in which I place tokens to remind me of His blessings; the hail is represented by a white rock in the appropriate size. Our grandson would often check out the many keepsakes in that basket and ask their meanings and I would explain them. One day he paused over the white rock and asked doubtfully, "Is this a true story?" I intended to do something significant with him that day; now I had my answer.

We drove the 40 miles to the exact spot of the store and reenacted the incident. The Lord had the highway clear so we could slowly go through the motions step-by-step.

Ben could see the parking lot and the road where the semis pulled out with me in the middle. He saw how the car slightly turned when I let go of the steering wheel and how it could have gone into one of the ditches on either side of the road. I showed him the pull-off spot where I praised the Lord and cried; this story was now a visual reality for him.

Praise the Lord for allowing me to imbue that blessed time in our grandson when he was 8. What a blessing for Ben to know his nana had direct protection from the hand of the Lord.

A Snowstorm to Remember
Helen Kennell

The wind was howling and rattling the windows in our old farm-house. We were experiencing a real blizzard. My brother, Bob, and I woke in the morning, scrambled out of our warm beds, and jumped into our ice-cold clothes. We heard the sound of unfamiliar voices in the downstairs kitchen. During the night, a busload of travelers was stranded at our house because the highway was impassable. A Greyhound bus was stuck on US 24 just in front of our home. What excitement! We had no idea what fun was in store for us.

While our mother was busy preparing food three times a day for all those travelers, our father was in the barn trying to keep the farm animals comfortable. Bob and I were bundled up and played in the snow. One of the travelers came outdoors to play in the snow with us. For two days he helped us make a snow house in one of those huge drifts. First, we dug out the snow to make a doorway and we kept on digging until we had made a large room. If we bent over a bit, we could walk right into that drift. Next, we made a window to let light inside and a snow seat that circled the entire space. his was beginning to look like a real house. After gathering some long sparkling icicles from the edge of the chicken house roof, we decorated our wonderful shelter.

Evenings we listened to our snowbound guests tell stories or we played board games. My brother and I liked to read our books, but because our family didn't have a lot of money, we didn't have very many books and the ones we did have were worn from loving use.

On the third day the road crews were able to hand dig the bus out of its entrapment and our home was empty of visitors. Bob and I missed our new friends, but we still had great fun playing in our snow house and adding all kinds of decorations made of cans and bottles that we found on a scrap heap out back.

Several weeks passed and one day a big heavy box was delivered to our home. It was addressed to Bob and me. The mailman had never before brought a package for us children. Who had sent it? What excitement! We tore off the packing tape and opened that wonderful surprise. A box of books! All kinds of books. Bible stories, adventure stories, animal stories. What a treasure chest! We would have entertainment for many days, but where did this bounty come from? When we read the return address, we discovered that the sender was a salesperson for a publishing company. It was our snow house friend!

Old Windmill Turns Again
Ethel Stutzman

I was the youngest of five children and didn't realize until later how my parents struggled through the Great Depression and Dust Bowl near Protection, Kansas. My father was a minister and a farmer—in that order—and times were hard.

I knew I was lucky to have a penny to tie in the corner of my hankie for Sunday school, but life for me wasn't all bad. There was always plenty of love, food to eat, and clothes to wear because Mother could sew just about anything from other people's old garments. But in 1941, after many years of dust storms and crop failures, my parents deeded their farm to the bank and moved to Ohio where everything was green and gardens produced well. We felt we had moved to the Garden of Eden.

Many years later, my husband, Dale, and I with our children visited the old home place in Kansas. It filled me with childhood memories and soon became a regular point to visit on our travels west.

Becoming more sentimental as I grew older, I longed to bring part of that farm home with me. After checking with the owner of the farm and tumbledown, abandoned house during one of our visits, Dale and I took the cistern pump and loaded it in our van. Nearby lay the remains of the windmill. Dale carefully dug the fins, tail and motor out of the sand and loaded them in the van also. The wooden tower had long ago rotted away.

Upon our arrival home, we set up the cistern pump as part of the landscaping in front of our house. It sat on a concrete slab with the words "THOU GOD SEEST ME" etched into the cement. Those were the same words Dad had inscribed on the cistern platform years before. Our place wasn't big enough for the windmill, so we had it erected on the Greencroft Goshen campus, which was home at one time to my father and older sister. It stands proudly on a lovely spot near a pond with ducks, geese and swans. A pavilion and picnic tables stand nearby, where folks can sit and view the turning windmill.

Imagine the thrill as I heard the wind turning the wheel for the first time in about 60 years. It brought back many memories, such as having the wind turn the wheel to fill the stock tank with water, chinning ourselves on the wooden bars, or placing a bolt on the pump so we could pump some water, which was always good and cold. It didn't come any fresher.

Several years after the windmill was erected at Greencroft, Dale and I moved to one of the courts located on the Greencroft campus. Along with many other seniors on campus, we can now enjoy the turning of the wheel in the wind. My family and I could not return to live at the home place in Kansas. So it makes it all the more special to have nearby the pump and windmill that faithfully provided our water during my childhood.

Not (Yet) Tuned In
David A. Shank

I have not forgotten the Sunday when Papa drove our family of seven children and Aunt Sallie in our old, air-cooled, seven passenger "Franklin" from 123 Wise Street in North Canton, Ohio, to church in Orrville. What made it particularly memorable was the after-church invitation to dinner at the Ben Geiser farm, where there were just about as many children as at our house. I recall nothing about church that Sunday, or the Geiser children, except maybe Doris who was about my age, and in my Sunday school class. I was about 6 or 7 years old. It was during the Depression, sometime during 1930-31. Papa was for Herbert Hoover; Ben Geiser was not. Ben was a farmer and needed help "from Washington."

The reason I remember all of this is because of the radio. I think it was the first time I had ever heard that word. Papa and his friend Ben were talking about "radio," and "ether waves," and "antenna," and "earphones," and other things that were all new to me, and quite strange. During the meal, it became clear that Papa and Ben were planning to "tune in," to the radio after lunch. I was very curious to see what in the world that would be like. I can't be sure today, but at that time, it seemed as though it was going to be a new experience for Papa, too. I could hardly wait for dinner to be finished for the "tune in."

After this big Sunday farm dinner, Papa and Ben took their chairs to and sat in front of a low table, on which there was a rectangular box, about two feet long and about as high as a man's hand, or a little more. On its front were what seemed like a number of round knobs, both big and small, along with what looked like several half faces of clocks, but each with only one hand. Those hands moved back and forth, pivoting from the bottom of what was the "dial," rather than going around from the center like a clock. Papa and Ben both put over their heads and ears what looked like metal earmuffs that had wires going over to the box.

Ben asked Papa if he was ready, and when he said that he was, Ben flipped a switch and the dials lit up. Then Ben started turning the knobs, with the hands on those half-faced dials going slowly back and forth, like he was trying to find just the right spot. Then he turned other knobs—or so it seemed—and went back again to the first ones, turning the knobs slowly, ever so slowly, until all of a sudden, he stopped very brusquely and straightened up.

"Do you hear that, Charlie?" he cried out. And I didn't hear anything at all, except Papa saying, "I hear it . . . like it's very, very far away." What was "that" and "it?" I wondered. How could one hear something far away coming from a box on a table? And Ben fiddled with the dials until Papa smiled again.

"It's coming from WADC Akron!" shouted Ben. "Once I even got WTAM Cleveland," he continued. How could that be? Our Uncle Roy, Mama's only—and younger—brother, lived in Akron. That was so far away that we didn't get to see him very often. So how could Papa and Ben hear whatever it was that was coming from far away Akron? They looked at each other, smiled, nodded, then looked puzzled, then smiled again. Through the earmuffs, they were clearly hearing something, somehow. I was left in the dark. I did not know what or how they were hearing anything. Today, I guess I would say I was "tuned out."

This strangeness of radio seemed clearly meant for grownups, so I went out to the barn to play. But all the way home to North Canton in that seven passenger "Franklin," all of the talk between Papa and oldest sister Ruth and brother Paul was about the new mystery–for me–of "radio." I gained a new word in my developing vocabulary that Sunday, one that still fills me with wonder.

Bittersweet Memories
Paula Stoltzfus

The big black wood-burning stove in the kitchen became a cozy warm place to be on cold days. As Mom baked good-smelling bread in the oven, she didn't mind having children playing nearby.

One time, fascinated, I watched my older brother Virgil use his jackknife on a stick of firewood from the wood box behind the stove. When I asked Mom for a knife so I could whittle, too, Mom said no and kept on washing the dishes. I watched and longed to have the fun Virgil had, thinking boys have all the fun. He put his knife down to go get a drink from the blue and white enamel water pail on the cupboard. I didn't stop to think, but grabbed his knife and stick and began to whittle as fast as I could.

I forgot to be careful when suddenly blood spurted over my hand, clothes and floor. A big slice of my middle finger came off with the wood. I screamed! Mom quickly put clean water into the basin and washed the blood off my hand. When the bleeding finally stopped, Mom poured red iodine over my finger. Then I yelled even louder because it hurt worse than a bumblebee sting. Next, Mom bandaged the cut finger and hugged me tight.

Later, I learned girls do have fun and can do all sorts of interesting things. Dressing up became really fun. A big gunnysack under the stairway held all the castoff rags. That's what mom called them. To me they offered many hours of entertainment. One day I found a pair of shoes with HEELS. When I slipped them on, I felt tall and queenly. True, many buttons had to be fastened over my ankles and up my legs, but they had HEELS. I didn't see anything odd in the fact they looked terribly out of style. I spent many happy hours wearing them.

Becoming obsessed, I begged Mom to let me wear the shoes to school. Finally, probably to stop my whining, she said yes. The glory lasted until time for first recess. Bob, the boy sitting in the front of me, glanced down and saw the ancient array on my feet. In an instant I went from bliss to sheer misery as Bob's loud laugh caught the attention of everyone in Miss Cusser's third-grade classroom followed with, "Hey, look at Paula's shoes." The enchantment disappeared. I never wore the heels again.

Learning how to work and help with chores came automatically. Dad introduced the first Allis Chalmers combine to Oscoda County, Mich., in time to harvest the oat field. I rode on a small platform on the right side near the back of the machine ready to tie the bags as they filled one at a time. Pulling a lever changed the flow of oats to the second bag. Then I had time to tie the first bag, pull it out of the way and put another bag on the empty chutes.

The machine was of great interest to farmers driving by on the highway. Many stopped to see how it operated. Dad patiently explained and showed them. I proudly showed my part from my spot where the chutes and bags waited. When Casper Bloomer, the friendly county agent, stopped to look it over, my proud moment expanded. It quickly deflated when he asked Sammy Troyer, one of the interested farmers who had climbed over the wire fence to observe, to take my place so he could take pictures of the operation. He told me to sit on the seat, making me just the kid watching all the action. Quite a few years passed before I learned to laugh at the humiliation I felt that day at the behest of the "friendly county agent."

Today, these bittersweet memories make me smile. I don't have a big black wood-burning stove in my kitchen, but I do enjoy the aroma of baking rolls and cookies with grandchildren stopping by to visit.

Embarrassing? Yes!
Roseanna Foley Maust

When I was a girl growing up, nearly every small town had a band-stand in the center of town, usually where the two main business streets crossed. A bandstand was a platform that stood about four feet above the ground. It had an open railing around it and a roof over the top. There were steps on one side to get on it.

The local musicians would get together and form a band. Then we would have band concerts with the musicians sitting on chairs on the bandstand. The concerts would often take place on warm summer Wednesday evenings. The farmers would finish their work early that day; the family would get cleaned up and everyone would go to town for the band concert. The women would sometimes bring their chicken eggs to sell and do their shopping, and the men would stand around and talk about the weather and their crops. The children would run and play and the older girls would walk in pairs around and around and look at the boys, and the boys would glance at the girls as they went by. It was a festive time.

One evening there was a talent contest to be held on Wednesday night on the bandstand. The neighbor lady asked my sister and me if we would sing and play the piano for the talent contest to represent Wabash Township. We had sung at church and at school, but we had never sung in a talent contest or played the piano for one either. The neighbor lady sounded desperate for someone to represent our township, so very reluctantly we agreed.

The day of the contest my sister and I had to help my dad plant tomatoes. Dad drove the horses that pulled the tomato planter and my sister and I sat down almost on the ground with big bunches of tomato plants on our laps. The machine was very unique. It dug a hole, squirted in water and white powdered fertilizer. Marvel and I took turns dropping a tomato plant in the hole and the machine pushed the soil around the plant. Of course, we got all covered with dirt and fertilizer and smelled like tomatoes.

When we got home, we had to really scrub ourselves and wash our hair. In those days we didn't have hair dryers or curling irons, so what to do with our hair was a big problem. We decided to wear our hair in turbans made with our matching scarves. Turbans were popular during the World War II years since many women had to wear them or snoods to work in defense plants. A snood was a long net, that held a woman's hair, and it had strings to tie on top of her head. That was so no woman's hair would get caught in machinery while she was working.

We wore matching summer suits and were all ready with our hair in turbans when the neighbors came to pick us up.

There were about eight or nine different acts in the talent contest. An announcer called us up one at a time when it was our turn to perform. The only thing on the platform was the piano.

We had chosen to sing the song, "Let's Remember Pearl Harbor," accompanied by the neighbor lady on the piano. I sang the melody and my sister harmonized with me. Then the neighbor lady left the platform and my sister and I sat down at the piano and played a duet, "The Church in the Valley by the Wildwood."

When it was all over, there was a period of waiting while the announcer went to get the winners' list from the judges. When the announcer came back, to our surprise he said, "The Foley sisters from Wabash Township have won first prize. Will they please come up to the platform?"

So, my sister and I wound our way through the crowd and went up on the platform. The announcer looked at us and said, "Excuse me."

He left us standing on the platform with everyone staring at us for what seemed like ages. That was embarrassing enough for two shy country girls. But when he came back, he said, "There has been a mistake. The (he named the other sister act) have won first prize." My sister and I slunk off the stage feeling very embarrassed and mortified. The other act was three little sisters who sang the same song, "Let's Remember Pearl Harbor," and in cute little outfits tap-danced.

As we walked through the crowd, some of the people said,"You girls did real good."

The neighbor lady who had asked us to perform felt very sorry for us and they gave us some money. But it wasn't that we expected to win or wanted to win. It was the embarrassment!

All for a Piece of Pie
Florence Nafziger

My family moved and lived in many different places, mostly on the
farm. My family at this time consisted of my parents, my two older
brothers, myself and a younger brother, We two were called "the children," which was a source of irritation to me. I felt that I should not
be classed with my brother who was five years younger! I also did not
want to be classed with my two older brothers who were four and
five years older than I. I wanted to be me.

Things came to a crisis when Dad planned to paste some wallpaper over the walls in the newly-added room. The big question was
who was going to get to help Dad paste the big pieces of exotic colored wallpaper, all smeared with lovely sticky paste? Now, at this
time, I realized that it should have been Chester, the neighbor boy,
who was my age, but a good deal stronger than I. But he was just my
age; what an insult. Chester's face lit up when Dad asked for his help
to do what I wanted to do. He was delighted to help and do a real
man's job.

But the effect on me was different. I was disappointed and angry.
Wasn't I as old as he? Why did my father pick him? I turned and
slowly walked away to a grassy shady spot where I could watch the
work being done without my help.

As the day wore on, I got tired and sleepy. Then I heard Mama
calling me to supper. The work looked pretty and Chester looked
very pleased with his part in it. Mama had saved a piece of pie for
me. As I began to eat, I decided that it seemed rather dumb of me to
waste a whole day being mad instead of watching the whole process
of making the room over to look like a palace in my eyes. I took a
big piece of pie and grinned. Compared to the heat and my spell of
anger, the pie was the top winner that day!

Childhood Magic
Reynold Sawatzky

In the late autumn of 1929 when I was a month less than 5 years of age, I rode with Dad to Richey, our nearest town, 17 miles from our rural parsonage in eastern Montana. There, in Pedersen's General Store, Dad gave Walter Pedersen a list of groceries and left me with a penny for candy while he took care of other business.

While serving another customer, Mr. Pedersen went into a back room and emerged shortly with a length of stovepipe. I naturally assumed that all of the wonderful merchandise on the high shelves behind the counter was made by Mr. Pedersen in that back room a Santa like magic workshop.

After that customer left, Mr. Pedersen was able to turn his attention to me. He smiled and tried to entice me closer to the candy behind the glass under the counter by pointing to various kinds and asking me to make a choice. I stood back entranced by Mr Pedersen's soft white hands. If he made stovepipes in that backroom, how was he able to avoid having any cuts from the sharp edges?

After Dad returned to pick up the groceries, and I finally had some candy, we left for home. There, I hunched down at the southeast corner of the parsonage and took another more insightful view of my surroundings. To the southeast Retah Table broke off at an angle from the northeast to the southwest in our pasture, and in that opening I could see across the broad valley with its lava mounds six miles to another table ridge where several dots represented Girlinger Ranch.

Standing away from the parsonage and sheds I could see the full circle of the high plains bare horizon. I believed I was seeing the whole world—a simple ideal world under the umbrella of the vast blue dome of sky. Although I could not see Richey to the northwest, I assumed that Mr. Pedersen with his magic workshop was within my world. The eastern Montana "House of Sky" greatly influenced my world in a unique way.

The economies in the world's financial capitals were collapsing and the Great Depression that would afflict us for the rest of my growing-up years would eventually crush my perfect world.

The Day the Gypsies Came
Jean Christ

Ten-year-old Ruthie Huffman hurried through her morning chores for she was happy. She was going to take care of Baby Mary, in her opinion the most beautiful baby in the world with her dark hair and big brown eyes. She was hoping to start sewing a dress for her baby sister, one of her favorite hobbies.

Her father, David Huffman, had taken his horse and mail cart to deliver mail on his route in the country. Her mother, Hettie, was working out in the field behind the barn. The neighbor lady knew Ruthie was the only one in the house taking care of Baby Mary. She had promised Hettie, Ruthie's mother, that she would keep an eye on their home.

Ruthie thought about the last place they lived–the Hubbard farm. It was a wonderful place and Ruthie was sorry when they moved. The big apple orchard across the road in front of the house provided the most delicious fruit in the late summer and fall season. All her life she would never forget the names of all these apples and their spicy or sweet juicy flavors and aroma.

The Huffman family loved to listen to the stories of old Mr. Hubbard as he told how he and his family used to hide up in the attic as they watched the Potawatomi Indians file by on the road in front of their farm. Indeed, Ruthie's daddy had a big box full of Indian arrowheads he had found when he plowed up the field across the Elkhart to Nappanee Road east of the farm where the Potawatomi Indians had often camped.

The dense woods in back of the Hubbard farm were frightening to Ruthie with all the creatures lurking there. She never went into those woods. It was thick, dark, and scary. Her Uncle Jasper had even seen a porcupine. That was the only place Ruthie did not like about the Hubbard farm.

But now the Huffman family had moved to the Rupert farm in Jimtown, and the fear that made Ruthie shiver this day was from the stories folks were telling about the gypsies. The gypsies were in Elkhart, too close for comfort! Many told stories about the gypsies stealing babies and raising them as their own children. Ruthie tried to forget about it as she started to work on Mary's new dress. Mary, with her dark hair and very dark eyes even looked like a gypsy!

All was quiet in the house, Baby Mary was sleeping upstairs. Ruthie gathered all her material to start working on the baby's dress. As she worked carefully, she began to hear some noise in the distance. She kept on working, until she noticed the din of many horses and wagons was growing louder. She glanced out the front door only to see to her surprise and alarm that it was gypsies, and they were stopping in front of their place! Several of the gypsies had hopped down from their wagons and were coming toward their house! What could she do? It was too late to go after her mother. She must not leave Baby Mary alone.

To her great fright and dismay, the gypsies came right on in the house. They were looking in the kitchen, taking bread and other food they found there. One of them said to her, "Do you have a baby here?"

"N-n-no," Ruthie answered. Oh, if only they don't decide to go upstairs and look, she thought. If only Baby Mary keeps on sleeping. Oh, she hoped the baby would not wake up and start crying.

Another sound was filling her ears now, and frightening the gypsies–an angry, barking dog. The neighbor lady had seen the gypsies stop at the Rupert farm. She immediately hurried over to the Huffman's home as fast as she could with her bulldog. The terrified gypsies fled out the door, back to the road and back to their caravan. The gypsies jumped into their wagons in great haste, and rushed away from the angry dog with a clattering and jangling. However, the bulldog managed to bite one of them and keep a souvenir of his ripped pants!

Ruthie was saved, and so was Baby Mary. By this time Mother had returned from the field, and the family was safe again. God had used a caring, watchful neighbor and an angry bulldog to come to the rescue. This was an event Ruthie never forgot. She told her children and grandchildren this story over and over in the years after.

Embroidery Lessons
Mary Elizabeth Martucci

Mom invited Cousin Rose to visit during summer vacation as her husband had gone overseas. Although my sisters and I were a bit younger than Rose, Mom thought she would be a good influence.

Rose was always lots of fun and never lacked good ideas to keep us amused. Of course, it was the 1940s and the war was on. Some might even say kids were more innocent or less creative then.

In those days, all girls knew how to sew and spent hours making items for their "trousseaus." "Hope chests" were in vogue, according to Rose. So, with Mom's approval, Rose initiated the embroidery lessons.

At Murphy's 5&10, the supplies were purchased for our embroidery of towels and pillowcases. Seeing the hoops, needles, skeins of brightly colored floss and iron-on designs, we were excited about the project.

After ironing on the design we had chosen, we selected colors of floss. I wanted only bright colors for my rainbow of flowers, but Rose (being more knowledgeable) added greens and browns, too.

We were seated in a row, project and supplies beside us on small boxes. Then, like a drill sergeant, Rose gave the commands. "Pick up hoop, place over area to be embroidered first, thread needle and knot." Getting on the hoops was a challenge, but making a knot was an even bigger one.

Next, we learned the various stitches called for in the design. Straight stitch was a snap. Satin stitch was even more simple. "This is really easy," I said smugly. But then came loops and French knots!

Rose was a great teacher. She watched us closely, not saying much to discourage us, and I felt sure I was mastering the task. Soon, Rose called a halt to the exercise and, like any good teacher, asked to examine our work more closely.

Rose commented on how well my sisters had done and made a few suggestions for improvement. I, on the other hand, brought frowns from Rose and gales of laughter from my sisters. "This is awful," said Rose. "There's nothing I can fix. Tear it out and start over!"

I laughed, too, and then said, "I quit." After all, it was supposed to be fun, not work. Who needed a trousseau anyway? I was 7 years old and didn't even know what it was!

But Rose would have none of that. Despite my protests and because of Mom's investment in the project, I didn't get off easily. Back I went to my task and tried again, and again. Finally, by late afternoon, I got Rose's approval. My sisters had finished their pieces earlier and were off playing elsewhere. My towel, literally damp and mutilated, equaled how I felt.

Today, I'm grateful for Cousin Rose's insistence that I learn to embroider. Surprising to me is the fact that I did continue to improve through the years and advanced to doing crewel, making wall hangings, pillows, tablecloths and napkins, and enjoying my hobby. My sisters gave up the project shortly after their first success.

How a Needle and Thread Changed My Life
Phillip C. Ross

It happened during World War II when I was in the Navy. My assignment at that time put me in charge of 60 women in a large warehouse at the Crane Ammunition Depot in southern Indiana, where I was one of only two males. My peers sure gave me a hard time kidding me about it.

A sailor friend was engaged to a girl who worked in the front office, with whom I came in contact to secure an OK to look at blueprints. To make a long story short, she and my buddy persuaded me to go with them on a blind date to meet her sorority sister. We were to meet at his fiance's brother-in-law's funeral home in Odon, Indiana (Poindexters, whose son was a figure in the Reagan Contra CIA affair) who were to be our hosts. We were to meet at 5:30 p.m. We were able to leave the depot early and arrived about 2:00 p.m.

Well, this caused a very poor beginning as the girls were out in the backyard sunbathing in some hand-me-down apparel and very embarrassed to meet us this unprepared way. I know that I had made a very poor first impression, and also felt that they had done an over-selling job on me, which did not help to impress her, as I could feel from her first reaction upon our meeting.

It so happened that I had ripped my uniform collar on our way, and after things settled down, the subject came up, as I apologized for my appearance. My date, Ruth, without hesitation, told me to take off my shirt. She took it into the home, and in what seemed like a very few minutes, came back out with it repaired looking like new. Well, believe it or not, right then and there that needle and thread incident caused me to fall madly in love and I wanted her to be my wife. As I look back, I fell in love without really seeing her, and I always say I'm also glad she was an attractive, blue-eyed blond.

Thank God I was able to get her to consent to a second date, but it took a lot of time to get her to agree to be my wife. We just celebrated our 61st wedding anniversary with our two wonderful children, with their spouses and four wonderful grandchildren. I owe a wonderful life to a needle and thread and a girl who was a wonderful seamstress from her 4-H training. By the way, she made our daughter's beautiful wedding dress.

Honeymoon Chicken House
Lois Stickel

The car was stagnant with thoughts as Ray's parents and I drove to the train station to meet our special soldier who was returning to us. It was September 29, 1946.

Ray's parents had their own thoughts while I, his bride, was thinking my own. He was a boy who left the farm to answer his call to duty. Now, he was a man returning home to pick up his life. Ray and I had married six weeks before he was drafted.

Backing up to Christmas 1944 . . . knowing he would be drafted soon, we became engaged with the thoughts of marriage after he would return home from his term of service. However, by February 1945, "young love" took over. We wanted to be together as much as possible In those "quaint, old-fashioned days," a respectable young lady did not follow her special service man from camp to camp without being married to him. With the war raging, and sensing his time as a civilian would soon be over, we had a very simple wedding February 18, 1945.

After being stationed at the camp where Ray received his training to be a clerk typist, he found a room for us in town. I soon joined him and found a job in the dry cleaners at the PX three to four evenings a week. On those days, we rode the bus back to town together after I got off work. He was allowed to come into town every evening and for the weekends. Just so, he was back at camp every morning for roll call. My days were spent exploring the town, visiting the library, reading and socializing with other military women living at the home where we were rooming.

While Ray was on final bivouac, World War II came to an end. Ray was given a three-week leave before being sent overseas.

We had been separated for a year now and each of us had very different experiences of life and were not the same idealistic, naive, dreamers we were a year earlier. Does he still love me? Will he want to farm for a living? Where will we live? These were some of the questions floating around in my head.

Waiting at the depot to see that bright round light coming down the track from Chicago seemed like an eternity. Finally, the engine came hissing by, stopping with the coaches in front of us. Soon we saw OUR SOLDIER coming down the steps. Rushing into his arms and being soundly kissed erased my doubts of love.

Three younger sisters waited at home for our return. We talked late into the night "catching up." It was soon learned Ray had no intentions of farming, but no idea of any vocation he wanted to pursue.

Not wanting to live with either of our parents, we went house hunting. We soon found out that servicemen who had returned within the past year since the war was over had rented or purchased all of the available housing. Not finding anything available, we asked around about other possibilities. We were told that some of the people were buying a little acreage and building a garage or a little house they could add onto, until they could build "bigger."

My brother, Wilbur, working for a hatchery man we had known for most of our lives, told us some folks were buying new Quonset hut chicken houses to live in until they knew what they wanted to do. He and his wife had just bought several acres and were going to

Quanset hut, first home for Lois and Ray Stickel.

put a chicken house on it to live in temporarily. That idea sounded quite good to us, and after telling Ray's parents about it, they suggested that if we wanted to do this we could put one of these Quonset huts across the drive from their house. There was a pump outside their back door as well as an outhouse for us to use. At least it would give us a start. And since we didn't know where we wanted to put down roots, it was exciting!

We purchased a 14 x 24-foot Quonset hut. Our work was cut out for us, as we would be building it ourselves. We divided it into two rooms and had it ready to insulate and seal by the time Ray reported to Fort Sheridan, Ill. for his Nov. 10 Honorable Discharge from the army. We were now ready to make our chicken house into a "honeymoon home."

Being eager to be by ourselves, we moved our meager belongings in before it was tightly sealed. The head of our bed was placed at the outside wall by the window. One night a snowstorm came up with a hard blowing wind. We were awakened by a cold mist in our faces. Pulling the covers higher we went to sleep again. The next morning I stepped into a puddle of water coming from under the bed.

Kneeling down to look, I saw, of all things, a snowdrift under the head of the bed. Our cold mist was blowing snow coming from around the window. A larger crack along the bottom of the window produced the snowdrift.

We now became very busy each evening after Ray returned from his job at a South Bend factory. After we got the inside sealed against the weather for further snowdrifts, Ray built cabinets around a corner and down the wall to the bottled gas range. He built a kitchen sink in the long side of the cupboard. He also partitioned one side of the bedroom for a closet, building shelves in the end close to the kitchen for a pantry and storage.

We heated with a fuel oil space heater placed beside the door to the bedroom to filter the heat into the bedroom. We now had a cozy little fully functional Quonset chicken house home.

September 1947 found us shifting our furniture around to make room for our baby bed. October 10, we brought our 3-day-old daughter home from the hospital!

Ray had been considering taking advantage of the G.I. Bill of Rights to get some further education or training. He decided to become an electrician and enrolled in Coyne Electrical School in Chicago. In February 1948, Ray moved to Chicago for this five-month course and would commute by train each weekend. After graduation, he was hired by NIPSCO at the Goshen station. We now had a focus of where to live. Ray and I started looking for housing in the Goshen area. Finding nothing suitable, we bought a building lot in a new subdivision along West Clinton Street. In April 1947, we had a contractor build a basement home to live in while we built the house as we could afford to.

We sold our "honeymoon chicken house" to my younger sister

and her fiancé who were soon to be married. They were moving it across the drive from her in-laws.

Ray and I found we didn't need a fancy new house full of lovely things to be happy. We did the best we could, with what we had to work with at the time, working together for a common goal, respecting one another's wishes, desires and dreams.

Be it ever so humble, there was no place like home!

Memory
Weyburn Groff

In circles of aging people one often hears regrets about the loss of memory. Of course, these are justified by the moments of distress and despair when we misplace things, when we miss a doctor's appointment, or when we fail to turn up for a coffee or dinner invitation. Embarrassing, yes.

But, really, I prefer to think of the memories that bring me pleasure or inspiration. For example, out of the blue, these memories came to mind.

One Christmas Day in a London Underground (subway) station, Thelma, my wife, and I met an older woman who was traveling alone. Thinking she must feel lonely, Thelma asked her something about how she was spending the day. She replied, "I'll be alone, but I have my wireless (radio), and I like me own company!" I have recalled this many times and shared it in conversation.

Sometimes when spring comes round and daffodils are in bloom, a few lines from William Wordsworth's poem, "Daffodils," surface. Remembering a "host of golden daffodils," he wrote:

> For oft when on my couch I lie,
> In vacant or in pensive mood,
> They flash upon that inward eye
> Which is the bliss of solitude;
> And then my heart with pleasure fills,
> And dances with the daffodils!

Visiting with our 18-year-old grandson, who is very much into math and physics, I made reference to Albert Einstein. I recalled how when I was a student at Princeton Seminary, I would meet this great scientist on his morning walks across campus. Somewhat awed, Peter asked whether I had talked with him. "No, but I probably greeted him with 'Good morning. sir.'" I think my stock went up with Peter.

Occasionally the memory of a teacher evokes an incident, insight or sentiment that I prize; that consoles or inspires. Miss Hedley, eighth grade, liked to give us assignments to memorize a special passage from a poem. These words come to mind from "The Burial of

Moses," by Cecil F. Alexander:

> God hath His mysteries of grace,
> Ways that we cannot tell,
> He hides them deep, like the secret sleep
> of him He loved so well.

Thank you, Miss Hedley, of Suddaby School in Kitchener, Ont., 1934.

In my boyhood years, my family lived on a farm near Waterloo, Ontario. It was during the Great Depression of 1929-1935. Pleasures were few, but occasionally we were favored with a newborn calf, and once a colt! On these occasions, our mother awakened us earlier than usual to see the newcomer. The delight of these events is vivid, and still brings good feelings.

Then, of course, there are memories from the childhood of our own four children. Each enriched my stock of stories with their spontaneous comments and observations.

Margaret, when 2 or 3, was studying a picture of her Grandpa Miller. "If I kiss on him here, will he feel it?"

One day Raechel at breakfast warned us, "One week in the year I get angry with everybody, and this is the week!"

Ed, about 5 (in India) decided that he would use his Christmas gift money from Grandpa Groff to buy our neighbor's calf. He thought it would make a nice pet. In the negotiations with our neighbor, he was advised to take the calf for a day by way of experiment. By the end of the day, he was ready to return the calf with this definitive comment, "It doesn't do anything!"

When we were leaving India, which had been home for 18 years, we were leaving behind our cherished Spaniel, Penny. Our friends, Mr. and Mrs. Root, were to be her adoptive owners, and we were assured of her good care. But as we set out down the road by foot to the bus, Cheryl, aged 9, expressing feelings of all of us, mused, "When Penny dies, will we come back for the funeral?"

Oft-repeated memories may sometimes weary others, but they never lose their color or charm for us. Our memory bank may not yield its riches on call, but given the right moment, in solitude or in company, it is there to savor and enjoy.

The Ol' Root Beer Barrel
Daniel Roll

The root beer barrel located on the southeast corner of Main and Sycamore Streets of my hometown, Elkhart, Ind., was a gigantic barrel some 20 feet high and 12 feet in diameter. It was painted bright glossy orange with the A&W logo on the side. Around the barrel were windows and a thick counter painted the same high glossy color.

It was a one-man show with the owner standing in the middle of the barrel near the tap that squirted out the beautiful brown elixir and yelling to the customers and asking what they wanted. The mugs were to his right in the big galvanized tub of water on steel legs separated into three sections: big, small and baby. He washed the mugs and then stored them in this shallow tub of water. He served the people at the counter with three or four mugs in each hand. The mugs would be dripping wet and the foamy head would be overflowing the sides.

My first memory of the root beer barrel was when I was 4 years old. My sister, Carolyn, was commissioned to take us youngest three to the park. Usually, we all started off walking north on Main Street with me holding Carolyn's hand. Jane would walk on the other side of me, and Mary would usually run on ahead. After a few blocks my legs would give out and Carolyn would be obliged to carry me the rest of the way. I would put my head on her shoulder and it wasn't long before I would be slumbering to the rhythm of her step. But my head would pop up when I would hear Mary's begging for root beer.

Carolyn was only 14, but she was tough-minded. "No root beer before we play!" Mary, only 6, might pout for a minute or two, but then turn and run up the bridge to our playground for the day, Island Park. Jane was 9 years old and she could take it. But me? I yearned for that root beer, longingly looking over my sister's shoulder until we were over the bridge and the root beer barrel was out of sight. But when it was time to leave the park, all Carolyn would have to say was, "Let's go get root beer." All of a sudden I had my legs back and I could run to the root beer barrel.

I hated the baby mugs! That was what I always got. Carolyn

would get a big one for a dime, and Mary and Jane would get a small for a nickel each. I would beg for more and Carolyn would share hers with Mary and me. I could not see over the counter, so Carolyn and Jane would take turns holding me up to see the man pour the root beer. Once he had to stop and go into the attic to fix something. Maybe he ran out of syrup or carbonated water. I was intrigued by that. I fantasized what it would be like to play up there inside a real barrel. Finally, my sister's arms would go limp, and I would be relegated to the ground to drink my baby root beer standing under the counter staring at the glossy orange staves of the barrel. After a hard day of play and a root beer that burned your nose and tasted like it had a hint of sassafras, I was sleepy. Carolyn got the unenviable job of carrying me ten blocks down main street back home.

The last time I visited the barrel I was 14, and my friend, Richard, and I were coming home from football practice at North Side School. We had done bear crawls and wind sprints all evening. I was dying of thirst, and I guzzled down two "big" ones, and so did Richard. I saw the owner grab a baby mug for a customer, and I teased Richard about having a baby one. We both laughed about it.

However, our laughter turned to sadness when the owner said that he might be closing for good. He did indeed close, and the barrel sat there closed for a number of years before it was torn down. A bank sits on that corner now, and I can never drive by without thinking of the root beer barrel and all of the sweet memories of drinking cold, frothy root beers.

The Two-bit Chair
Robert Edwards, Sr.

Many years ago, I had my two youngest children with me when I stopped on a Saturday at a small auction house during a summer rain shower. Of course, the kids were less than excited about it, but had no other choice. We had to stand since there were no seats in the building. They were auctioning off most anything, even small pieces of stove pipe. They put up for bid an old rickety wooden folding chair that they finally sold to a man for 25 cents. I thought it wasn't worth even 25 cents. "He must be pretty stupid to pay that much for a 'worthless' chair," I thought to myself. It was only when the auction ended after two hours and everyone started to leave that I noticed the man who had bought the chair simply got up and left it behind. He had sat during the auction while everyone else had to stand.

Church – Dull?
Marjorie Banman Neufeld

For 15 years, from age 5 to age 20, my family resided in an aging, over-crowded, white frame, two-story house next to our church. The two upstairs bedrooms each had one window, the south one overlooking the road to the cemetery, and the north bedroom window with a view of the garden and the wheat fields flourishing in summertime.

The Banman sisters, top, left: Marjorie, Lela. Front, left: Joan, Elaine. Elaine, the youngest sister, died in 1993.

The two-story Alexanderwohl Mennonite Church on Highway 15 in central Kansas rises majestically above the surrounding well-kept farm buildings. It was built shortly after the General Conference Mennonites arrived from Russia in 1874, a testimony to the importance placed on a meetinghouse. These early pioneers would have been appalled by the behavior of the church janitor's four daughters—during non-church hours.

A short walk took us to the spacious wooden house of worship, which on Sunday drew a crowd of nearly a thousand. The church featured balconies on three sides, stained glass on all the windows, a long blonde finished wooden stage in front with a pulpit in the center, a piano to the left, and three high-backed wooden leather-cushioned chairs with armrests directly behind the pulpit. (Sometimes three ministers preached.) Steps on either side of the stage led to four graduated rows of 60 seats occupied by the choir. A Hammond organ was installed in the early 1940s and was placed to the left front of the choir loft.

What a setting to play church during the week! The pulpit, the stage, the piano . . . it was all ours! We preached with zeal, reaching high crescendos, and we waved our arms enthusiastically when taking on the role of song leader.

But, there was one problem. We were, after all, expected to dust pews, children's tables and chairs in Sunday school rooms, and mop floors. In our view, our whole family were underpaid, overworked "slaves." Sometimes, Dad, who was also organist and choir director, would practice on the organ while we worked. Surely, if he could sit and play the organ, we should not be denied a little diversion.

One such diversion had us checking the hymnal racks for expired Sunday school quarterlies. Since these were being discarded anyway, why not sail them down from the balcony toward the stage? It became somewhat of a competition, requiring considerable skill and energy.

Our creative play required no money, only imagination, including, one time, a three-way commentary on a funeral procession that smoothly led to our playing a wedding.

During the trek to the cemetery, observant bereaved individuals might have noticed three pairs of eyes peering through the screen of a slightly raised window. A roller shade was drawn to within inches from the bottom of the sill. We three girls, Lela, Margie (me) and Joan, viewed the unfolding drama while kneeling side-by-side as comfortably as possible.

We curious sisters observed the slow procession approaching from the church parking lot, heading east toward the cemetery, and passing only a stone's throw from the janitor's residence and the south windows. The hearse led the mostly black-clad mourners and a smattering of younger people and small children. The well-traveled road from the church to the cemetery, though unpaved, was well graveled to ensure "unmuddied" access due to frequent funerals. Imagine the scene.

"See the gray coffin in the funeral car?" The eldest sister broke the silence.

"Yep. There are lots of flowers on top of it," piped up number two, Margie.

"Hey look! That tall man in the black suit must be the husband of the lady who died. He is walking behind the ambulance," a third voice, Joan, added.

"And there are some moms and dads with children. Do you think those are the grandchildren?" asked Lela, the oldest.

Relatives and friends continued to come on the scene. Lela, Joan and I took it all in, mouths open and eyes following the parade.

"I've seen some of these people in church," I announced.

"Here comes a car with old people." Pausing, Lela added, "Probably it is too far for them to walk."

"This sure is a long pro-pro-motion." Being the youngest, Joan was losing interest.

"No, no. You mean 'procession,'" both older sisters corrected.

"Oh, yeah," Joan agreed.

When only a few stragglers remained in the line, a new idea emerged. "When everyone leaves the cemetery and people go home after the funeral dinner, let's go look at the grave and all the beautiful flowers."

"Good idea," agreed the other two.

I don't remember any reprimands from parents. It seems there might have been some, had they been aware of our intention of "borrowing" some of the floral beauties for upcoming nuptials.

And we DID stage several weddings! Knowing where to procure flowers for the occasion presented a challenge. You simply cannot have a wedding without flowers. The most resourceful member of our sisterhood suggested, "What about some of the flowers on the grave of that lady who was buried several days ago?" The cemetery extended as far east of our house as the church extended west. We could run right over and retrieve a few of the less than fresh flowers.

"But that would be stealing!" remarked little Joan.

Perhaps the majority ruled. The wedding went on as scheduled, flowers and all. The bride was adorned in lacey old curtains. The groom wore a white shirt, an oversized man's suit with the pants rolled up, and a bright tie haphazardly tied. The third person, likely Lela, read the vows, after considerable discussion as to which role each would play. Maybe Dad played the wedding march. After all, he did have a sense of humor.

Sunday morning church was never this much fun!

The Story Behind the Mirror
Esther B. Yoder

My 6-1/2- year-old granddaughter, Amber, and her mother and I were sitting in our living room cutting paper dolls. Amber looked up at the large mirror on the wall and asked where we got it. I said, "Oh, Amber that mirror has a story behind it and I'll tell you all about it." So I went into great detail to tell her about the mirror.

"Our son and his wife had purchased a home and this mirror was on the wall of the living room. When I found out that they did not want it, we purchased it and brought it home and Grandpa hung it on the wall, and that is where it has been ever since."

When I finished my detailed story, she looked up at me and said, "Grandma, could I see the story behind the mirror?" My daughter and I had a good laugh and then explained the meaning of the saying "The story behind the mirror." As I thought about this story, I had to wonder what kind of story is behind my reflected life.

First of all: Am I telling the story behind my mirrored life? Am I a woman who reads the Bible daily so that I know and live the Word of God?

Second: Does my life, as a mirror, reflect a woman who is peaceful and content because all has been shared with God in prayer? Has the Holy Spirit filled me anew each day so that I can meet whatever comes with love, joy and peace?

Third: Do I reflect a life that is standing firm on the rock, Jesus Christ? Is my faith in God evident to those around me? Can I stand beside someone who is weak and support them in their hour of need?

Fourth: Is my reflection different from the reflection of the world? Do I walk as Jesus walked? Do I meet people and circumstances with an attitude of love? Do I speak and act as one who wants to serve others?

Fifth: Do I reflect in my mirror a person who truly cares and loves? Do I have a compassionate heart toward all I meet? Do I take time to listen and then pray with the one who is joyful or the one who is hurting?

Sixth: Do I talk about the story behind my life? Do I tell people about the change Jesus makes? Do I really want others to experience eternal life with God?

Seventh: What kind of attitude do I reflect? Is it an attitude of thankfulness? Do I share willingly and joyfully of my time, talents and money? Am I seen as a giving person?

In conclusion, I want to reflect the life of Jesus in the mirror of my life. I can do this only if I live a disciplined life given over to the leading of the Holy Spirit. I challenge you. Do you want people to know the story behind the mirror of your life? Are you willing to share it?

Exodus 12:4: "Now go, I will help you speak and teach you what to say." (NIV)

A Snowy Winter's Day
Betty A. Kidd

The Lord blessed me with an exceptionally terrific grandmother. Seems she always busied herself doing for others after Grandpa's death. Friday was baking day. Rolling out pie dough was my favorite chore, while she opened the cans of red cherries or mixed together her delicious pumpkin spice recipe. Unless I put a bid in for my own little cherry pie (which was most of the time), the others went to a convalescing friend, other family members, the pastor, or a neighbor in need of a cheery hello.

Through the week, I enjoyed riding Dad's old black bike to the local grocery store for Grandma or Mother. However, this physically demanding activity began taxing my young body, as my anemic condition began to control every aspect of my life. More frequent than not, moments after entering the market, physically drained and exhausted, I often found myself groping for a shelf or something to steady my fall, as that frosty cold feeling settled around me and sounds faded from reality. Times, as I regained consciousness, a customer would be scrambling down the aisle to retrieve the rolling cans, or sweeping up particles of a broken flour sack I had fallen into. My presence was not always a welcome sight for the neighborhood grocer.

As I grew and developed, walking became my most physical activity, leaving Dad's trusty bike leaning against the wall of the timeworn tool shed. It was difficult to see my dusty old friend become such an excellent dwelling place for spiders and their next meal.

Winter was usually a good season for me physically. Times of exhaustion were less frequent, because I didn't have to fight the humidity and heat. Harsh winters in northern Indiana were nothing unusual; however, during the course of the night old man winter paid us a special visit. Grandma was up several times to rekindle the old coal stove, as the howling winds shuffled her lacy white curtains, and the blustery snow begged entry into every crack and corner of the house.

The entire landscape seemed to have changed during the course of the night. Tree branches dropped as the falling snow clung heavily onto their creaking outstretched arms. Houses securely wrapped in a blanket of snow seemed to snuggle a little closer to the earth, as smoke spiraled from their chimney tops, ensuring extra warmth. Fence and shrubs that once separated two houses were barely visible as the gusting winds whipped and formed a barricading wall. Burdened telephone wires swayed back and forth as if to rid themselves of the extra weight that was stretching their endurance.

As I trudged from Grandma's that Sunday morning, I wondered if the old blue church bus would make it to my house. Finally, the outline of home came into view. How beautiful the ice-laden river was that flowed behind our house! I paused, briefly, to listen to the gurgling water flowing between the buildup of ice and snow along its banks. Mother could hardly believe her eyes as I walked through the door, asking why I would venture out in this inclement weather. Clumps of snow fell to the floor as I unwrapped Grandma's cumbersome plaid scarf from my cold cheeks, to explain that I didn't want to miss the church bus.

I had no sooner entered the living room than I began to experience that overwhelming fatigue, as that cold frosty feeling engulfed my body once again. Barely making it to the couch, I fell unconscious. I remember thinking, "It's so dark in here; I've got to get up and get some air!" Struggling a little, finally turning myself around, I sat up with my feet securely on the floor. Momentarily gazing out the picture window, I marveled at God's beautiful winter's handiwork.

Mother was finishing the breakfast dishes about the time my little sister came out of our bedroom. Sis called to Mother, "Mom hurry; Betty fainted again. Get a cold washcloth!" I didn't think the alarm in her voice was at all justified under the present circumstance. Why would she tell Mother I had fainted when she could see perfectly well I was okay now?

It was then I noticed that she wasn't looking at me, but my body! I glanced to my right to see my legs hanging over the edge of the sofa. Startled, I turned back to my left to observe my body, lying face turned downward into the back of the cushions. What was happening? I was no longer confined to that fragile, feeble structure! I felt so weightless and full of life! My mind quickly raced back to that chilly fall morning when once before Father God had called for me to fellowship with Him. Excitedly, I wondered if I was going to walk and talk with Him again?

About that time, I heard Mother call my name, as she applied the wet washcloth to my face. She told me I was cold and white as a sheet, and "even if the church bus makes it to our house today. I think you need to stay home." How could I tell her what had just happened to me again? I had never heard anyone talk about leaving their body.

Excerpted from a book Betty Kidd is writing, *Called to be a Witness*

Papa, Please Don't Cry
Martini Reimer Janz

When I had just turned 5, my favorite person in the world died. It was my Grandmother Reimer.

At the time, we were living in a small western Manitoba town called Sperling. A long-distance call came from Steinbach to Sperling's red brick telephone office on Main Street. A messenger went to find my father and tell him to come to the telephone office for a message. After receiving the message, Father came straight home and began to speak quietly yet urgently with Mother. We tried to listen but we couldn't understand what he was saying. For my father to come home in the middle of the afternoon, we knew that something was wrong. He then just sat down, deep in thought, staring into space.

Mother told us we needed to hurry up and get ready to drive to Steinbach because our Grandmother Reimer was very ill.

Quickly, Mother pumped some water out of our basement cistern and placed it on the cook stove to heat. When it was hot enough, Father brought in our round wash tub and placed it in the middle of the kitchen floor. Mother was very particular that we all be spanking clean when we went to see our relatives, most especially the Reimer family aunties. Naomi, our oldest sister, took her bath first. She was already 12 years old. Next came Wendy, who was only 10. Then it was Betty's turn. She was 7 years old. Finally, it was my turn. I had just turned 5. Last of all, mother bathed our little sister, Hildie. She was our baby. She was 3 years old.

Of course, we all bathed in the same water since water was very scarce in western Manitoba where we lived. However, Mother was always very particular about our hair. She always kept back some of the clean warm water to which she added vinegar before she rinsed our hair. She knew it would make our hair shine. We quickly dressed in our best "small Sunday" clothes. Our mother sewed all of our clothes. In our family, we had "grand Sunday" clothes, "small Sunday" clothes, and "everyday" clothes. We dared not mix them up. Mother won blue ribbons for her sewing almost every year at the Carmen Fair.

To get to Steinbach we had to cross the Red River on a ferry at Aubigny. Mother was terrified of ferries. It had to do with an incident early in their marriage, when the ferry they were on nearly sank. So she always made sure that we were totally "ready" to go to heaven before we ever crossed any ferry. After crossing the river, Father drove as fast as the roads allowed. Soon we drove up to Grandmother's big yellow house on Main Street, right in the middle of the village.

We were strictly reminded to go into the house very quietly to meet the family and hopefully to see grandmother. We met the cousins, the aunts, and the uncles in the big front hallway. Everyone was so quiet. It was frightening to me. We watched Mother and Father go into the sewing room, just beyond the living room. Grandmother's bed had been moved from upstairs to the sewing room. Our Aunt Margaret told us that Grandmother had suffered a stroke (we had no idea what that might be). She told us to go out into the backyard and play with our cousins.

I didn't go. I snuck partway up the staircase because I knew that you could see into the sewing room through the transom above the door. A chair lay sideways in the bed. This seemed so strange. I could mostly see only the backs of my uncles and aunts gathered by the bed. I could not see Grandmother. I waited quietly and when Father came out he was crying. I had never in my life seen him cry. During that night, Grandmother died and went to heaven.

The evening before, the aunts had prepared a place for all the girl cousins to sleep. It was upstairs. The girls were in one room and the boy cousins in the other room, close by. My oldest cousin, Adeline, 18 years old, was so grown up and beautiful. Sleeping in the same room, I felt like I was sleeping close to a movie star.

The next morning they told us that Grandmother had died and gone to heaven. I was unable to grasp what had really happened. After we ate our store-bought cereal for breakfast, always a very special treat at Grandmother's house, we were sent out to play. I came back in and noticed that the dining room door was ajar. I peeked in and saw my grandmother lying on some boards placed over the table. Aunt Margaret actually mostly hid her from my view, but I could see that Aunt Margaret was washing her and crying bitterly. Just then my Uncle Jacob came by and noticing the door ajar, closed it and sent me out to play.

Then they took Grandmother away and brought her back within a day or so. Now she was lying in a beautiful black box that they had placed beside her living room bay window where she kept all her winter flowering plants. I learned later that my grandmother had the first store-bought coffin in the whole village. Just like always, my grandfather sat right beside her in his captain's chair. This Reimer grandfather never talked to us children, but we were used to that. So it seemed almost normal. Grandmother, in her rocker, beside Grandfather, used to talk a lot. Sometimes she would sing. She loved to tell us stories and always loved to laugh a lot, too. But not now. She was so still.

When the grownups went into the kitchen for coffee, I picked up a little stool to stand on so I could see Grandmother from up close. I put my little hands on the beautiful satin cloth that lined the coffin and watched and watched and waited.

I just knew that if I watched long enough, she would breathe again. Why, we had seen her take naps lots of times. Every day right after lunch she took a nap on the divan in the dining room. Grandmother always said that we could still play tag, or even play school on the stairs or blind man's bluff in the hall upstairs, while she napped. She said we could even watch her sleep, but we were not to touch her face because that would wake her up. We loved to watch her sleep because she made little bubbly sounds with her mouth.

I knew that if I watched long enough, she would do it again. I wanted to be the one who would run through the house and tell everyone that she wasn't dead anymore. Tell them not to cry anymore because she has come back. Come back from heaven to love us all again, just like she always did.

My father found me there and gently took my hands off the edge of the coffin and lifted me into his arms. He was crying, again. I was very sure that something really serious had happened in our Reimer family. It seemed like everything we loved so much had somehow changed. I sensed a "light" had gone out. Only later, and with tears of my own, did I come to know how right I was.

Life is a Dance
Tillie Nauraine

Act I
The opening movement was filled with thunderous pain, tears and longing. The dance moved through trees, gardens, lanes, meadows and twisted patterns. Sometimes the dance slowed to a brief respite of beauty, moonlight and hope. It lasted for 21 years and laid foundations for future resonant steps.

Act II
This dance rose and lifted as if from ashes and wound through a labyrinth of pages, a grasp of the ancients, a tender, satisfying awareness. A light from heaven, knowledge and greater wisdom, like diamonds to be treasured, were laid at my feet and I danced more lightly, with fervor and grace that was no less than divine.

Act III
This dance moved in lighthearted steps, but also had interludes reminiscent of the first act. The brightest score was filled with flying steps of little feet and music that circled and soared like wind laden with the fragrance of springtime, a celestial gift, lithesome and swift. The closing movement was a painful dirge that led to light and a forward step to the future.

Act IV
The pace of this score quickened with a dance that circles a mountain of dreams and visions of beauty. The quest for beauty reached a crescendo of brush strokes like a painted sunset of warmest colors and lasting grace and gratification. The grand finale is a slow dance that sweeps forward in a lyrical cadence of peace, acceptance and love.

Although the dance of life is an unknown score at the beginning, it can be deciphered and performed with divine grace, wisdom and joy.

Goshen and the Happy Sounds
Jack E. McKeever

Bells etching by Betty Jean McKeever.

Every town has distinguishing sights and sounds. In the middle 1920s sounds were quite different from today. The air was filled with the sound of bells. At least ten churches had belfries that pealed out every Sunday to call their parishioners to worship.

Each bell had a distinctive tone . . . so distinctive that you could tell which sexton had forgotten to check his watch. From a single isolated solo to a full voiced melody, the chimes rang from all corners of the city. What a glorious, happy symphony of sound. However, the bells that really let us know they meant business were the bells in the clock tower at the county court house.

Not only did it boom forth the hour, but also ran a series of greetings each quarter-hour. If you listened carefully, you could almost hear the echo of the four-faced clock hung on the corner of the City National Bank at Main Street and Lincoln Avenue.

Of course, there were other bells that were used as a warning as the city streetcars passed by and if the interurban was threading its way down Main Street. Then again, there was the bell on Mr. Blough's horse-drawn ice cream cart. It let the children know that goodies were passing their doors. At times, we could hear the bell of the railroad engine as it sat panting at the station. This locomotive also brought with it the sigh of steam and the smell of a hot boiler as the safety valve dropped the boiler pressure.

Then there was the frantic jangle of the fire equipment as the ladder trucks and pumpers rushed to the point of conflagration. Our life was not only controlled by bells, but it was enriched greatly by the sound of bells pealing in the night to let us know that all was well in our fair little city. Listen, you may still hear them echo.

We still have a few churches that peal the tower bells. It brings back memories . . . soothing sounds amid the cacophony of background noise. A reminder that bells are still pealing forth sounds of joy.

Jack McKeever died Oct. 2, 2007. Besides writing, his artistic pursuits included sculpture in metal, wood and marble, as well as painting. For 10 years after retirement he was a social worker and teacher's aide for at-risk and dysfunctional children, both in Napa County, Calif. and the Center for Community Justice in Elkhart County, Ind. His piercing eyes, deep voice and no-nonsense, but playful, demeanor revealed a man of character and compassion. He truly enriched others. For the majority of his career, Jack worked in manufacturing and engineering with most major aircraft companies.

Judge's comment: What an enjoyable piece! It's not a story, exactly – there is no conflict or resolution – but it's an excellent example of a descriptive memory. You know how to write. Every description is specific. Verbs are strong. Sentences are varied in their openings and lengths. And through it all, you capture a significant and interesting memory.

Part 2: Poems

Old Age
Helen Alderfer

Tread carefully, Helen. This is new ground.
This is not the childhood you survived,
not the turbulent years of youth,
not the desert places of middle years.
This is a land of new rules:
Do not give advice, even when asked.
Do not tell the old stories over and over.
Do not recite your ills. They are dear only to you.
Do not ask people to speak up,
for they say they are not speaking more softly than before.
And do not ask them to repeat
(not all they say is worth repeating. . .).
Be cheerful. Smile when they say you are exceptional.
Take the arm that is offered, the best seat that is given you,
the doors that are held open.
Remember, you are a pioneer with a frontier to be crossed.
You are traveling with the young and those who would be young,
who do not know that they will get old.
When you are alone you may talk to yourself,
sing a few bars of Aida,
twirl a few dance steps while the tea water boils.
But only if you are alone.
Pray for grace.

First place
*Judge's comment: What I like best about this wise poem is its compelling
"voice" and successful use of extended metaphor.*

Ode to the Pacific
Verna Birky

There's a silence in the roaring thunder of the sea
As she flings her breakers crashing on the rocks
And spews the briny foam along the sandy shore.

There's a silence as the gulls obey her call
And nestle down to feed upon her gentle, rocking breast,
While she cradles yet more life unseen below
Safe within the secret bosom of the deep.

We who love her also know her nurture and caress
As she offers us that bounty of her store.

But there's silence as her icy fingers claim another person,
unwary of her unforgiving rage.
"She's a traitor," are our thoughts.
"She has robbed us."
Stunned and silent, we cannot speak aloud the words
for her to hear as we cling to those about us
In our unbelieving grief and angry fear.

There's a silence as I stand at water's edge,
The now spent waves lap gently on my toes.
I gaze in silence at the far-off blue horizon.
There are no words to share my long intrigue
Of her majesty and unrelenting might.
Restless, never sleeping through infinity of time.
I ponder this unchanging, raging thing
That sustains life, then snatches it away,
Whose wrath mere humans cannot find control.

I linger briefly on her gently sloping shore
As she tugs the sand from underneath my feet.
Then in silence and in mystery I worship
Our creator God, the one who made us both.

Poet's comment: A native Oregonian, my "love affair" with the mighty Pacific ocean began as far back as I can remember. We lived on a farm about 75 miles from the coast. After the harvest was done, and if there was enough time before school started, our family would take a few days off and go to Newport, where U.S. Highway 20 ends. There we enjoyed "God's crowning work of creation." What fun it was going deep sea fishing, digging clams, investigating tide pools, building sand castles, whale-watching, eating seafood, being aware of a glorious sunset and hearing the ocean's roar lulling me to sleep at night.

Second place
Judge's comment: This poem finds music in language and ambitiously tackles a difficult theme.

Tea Country
Areta G. Lehman

Pulsing green
Stretching,
Undulating
To the high horizon.

Potent mix
Of golden sun
And azure wash
In heaven's bowl.

Then hands reach
To pluck the verdant bud
Rhythmic fingers stretch
To pinch a living
From the living green.

Now I dream
Above a cup of chai,
Careless
Of the lonely toil
That cheers my day.

Third place
*This poem was written April 4, 1998 in Shirati, Tanzania, after a trip
to Nairobi. We had driven through tea country (elevation 5,000 feet)
near Kericho, Kenya. The rolling hills were a brilliant yellow-green and
the plants (of the camellia family) were pruned to the picker's height.
Under heavy leafage grew the knobby shrubs, perhaps 100 years old.
Tiny villages of the tea pickers were nestled in the fields, far from the city.*

*Judge's comment: Each word in this imagistic poem is carefully chosen
and helps paint a memorable picture.*

Hope's Haiku
Hope (Diamond) Bartlett

We, like leaves . . . dry . . . fall.
Following same life cycle . . .
Soon . . . gone with the wind.

Energy and life . . .
The most precious gifts of all.
Synonymous terms.

Some guilty pleasures:
Dancing to Fifty's music . . .
Lemon meringue pie!

Friends share joys/burdens.
Doubling . . . vicariously . . .
Pleasures and comfort.

Precious grandchildren.
Our final reward on earth?
What a way to go . . .

Relics from My Attic
Royal Bauer

With a slight brushing away of the cobwebs
in the attic of my memory
What pictures are hung there
Of days long past?
Cisterns and the pitcher pump;
The two-holer with the Sears catalog;
Kerosene lamps, with wicks that needed trimming
And chimneys that needed cleaning with crushed newspapers;
Later, the Aladdin lamp with its bright mantle;
Dark cellars of fruit and vegetables in bins;
Wood boxes, cob bins, and coal buckets that forever needed filling;
The reservoir on the range that supplied warm water;
The galvanized tub brought in for the Saturday night bath;
The truck patch with its tenacious weeds;
The De Laval cream separator;
The ABC (Altorfer Bros Co) hand-operated washing machine;
The cider press and grindstone, each
Needing a boy like me to do the turning.
Me, with an attic full of memories
Loads more than these,
Grateful for a steadfast God
Who gives meaning to life
Amid all the changes.

Madness
Luke Birky

There is an illogical madness in birthing.
Love brings new life through labor and pain.
The finest minds and skilled hands aid.
Awe, respect, love increase.

There is an illogical madness in war.
Fear and greed bring conflict, war – human against human.
Cluster bombs, uranium tipped bunker busters destroy, maim and
    kill.
The finest minds and skilled hands aid.
Awe, fear, smoldering hatred increase.

The invitation remains: "Choose life."

The Window
Nadine Corse

As I sit by the window . . .
and wait
the state of the world I contemplate.
Be it love or be it hate.
As I once sat by that window and waited.
Was it love I was searching for?
Or was it truly something more?
As I sit by the window and wait,
I realize that what I'm truly seeking
Is not something outside, inwardly speaking.
But something planted within by the creator of all creators
who says, Woe to those in the vast sea of hateful haters.
By that window, I will no longer wait, watching
the best of my life, the world to take.
A choice is mine to make,
be it love or be it hate.
My own road I choose to take.
And traveling on it, will be great!

*I wrote this poem after my first husband decided to go wandering off on
his own. The thoughts and feelings helped me realize my own value and
to move on.*

Kentucky Winter 2007
Sandra A. Fryer

Hills laden with snow
chills of 6 below,
Temperatures sustained at zero.
Icy, shimmering trees glisten in the sunlight.
Dripping icicles hang from lawn chair backs.
Four days go by and Kentucky rains come hurling down.
Natural streams through yards and hills carry away crystal snow.
Here we are inside, with another log to stoke the fireplace glow.

A Grandmother
Doreen Geary

Is like a secret agent
Assigned
And hell bent on breaking
All the rules
With grandchildren.

We laugh
And giggle together
At Mom and Dad
Who are way too earnest.

On a car trip,
I pop gum with them
While their dad tosses me
(you should know better)
Looks.

I continue
Holding down time
As long as I can
Wishing
The summer would last forever.

Joy After The Storm
Georgia A. Gill-Elkins

A storm wandered in, lasting the night
Morning dawned with a gray, dismal sky.
Drizzling rain clouds still lingered
As I arrived at my son's house.
Breaking clouds allowed the sun to shine through
On puddles scattered upon the yard.
Along the drive the silent faces of my grandsons greeted me,
Their laughter and shouts of delight
Caught our attention as we turned our heads.
We watched the boys splash through puddles.
Then the youngest laid down in the middle of the muddiest,
Laughing and rolling in the mud.
Watching him, I remembered the fun I had as a child.
I never liked thunderstorms,
But when the fear of the storm passed
All the lightning was forgotten
And I, too, loved to play in puddles.
Watching my grandson rolling in mud,
Reminded me that even though storms of life
Oft fill the skies,
When they are past,
There will be puddles wherein we can rejoice.

What Are You Doing With Your Dash?
Chuck Hernley

A cemetery is adorned with many a stone.
One can find last names from Abraham to Zone.
Some stones tremendous, others of modest class,
Friend, what are you doing with your dash?

Regardless the size, always inscribed here,
Your date of birth, the dash, the death year.
Are you living flamboyantly, lots of panache?
Friend, what are you doing with your dash?

Are we doing the work God's called us to do?
Living the Christian life each year we pass through?
Do our thoughts and actions with others clash?
Friend, what are doing with your dash?

Habits reveal our character as we get older in life
Do we waste energy with worry and strife?
Are we consecrated in prayer, or is our prayer list stashed?
Friend, what are you doing with your dash?

When that day comes and our dash is complete,
We pray that God's purpose on earth we did meet.
As we kneel in His Presence, our life will flash.
Friend, we'll know what we did with our dash!

I wrote this poem after attending Promise Keepers in Indianapolis and hearing a speaker talk about walking through a cemetery and noticing the dates and dashes, wondering if he is living his dash the way he should. I hope my dash will mean something to somebody, 1930 – .

Ghana
Laurence M. Horst

Enchanted land of diamonds,
Rich and rough and rare.

Wealthy land of minerals,
Entrusted to her care.

Famous land of cocoa.
Around the world is known.

Inuit eating chocolate bars,
Which are "Ghana grown."

Forests of mahogany,
To grace the global mart,

Are grown here in Ghana,
And to foreign ports depart.

Delicious fruits of Ghana,
To bring good health to all.

The gardens of Aburi,
Reveal to small and great

The natural wealth within
This potent Black Star State.

The Storm
Katherine Johnson

Who has not wakened in the night, to listen, intent,
to sound not repeated but recalled?
There! It comes again.
A distant rumble from eastern hills.
Earth holds its breath as time stands still.
Soon cooling breezes stir the night, bringing fat drops
to splash upon the leaves and thirsty ground.
And then the waited deluge,
pounding the rooftops, fields and swollen streams. All nature shouts
with gladness for this abundant blessing
until, as morning approaches, the storm gives up its hold and rumbles
to the West.
And the earth, renewed, awaits the Rising Sun.

The Puzzle
Lola M. Kauffmann

Quietly she sat,
Her brown eyes watching me.

I stood at the table,
Working on a 1,000-piece puzzle.

She hardly knew me
As we lived miles apart.

She was only three,
I, her Grandmother.

She rose and pushed a
Chair for me to sit.

Surprised by her caring,
I said, "Why, thank you!"

With a grin, she returned to her seat,
A piece of our puzzle put in place.

My Mother's Apron
Lila Miller

When I was just a little girl
And I'd begin to cry,
My mother took her apron
And wiped the teardrops from my eye.

But now that I am older
And slacks are all the dress,
How do mothers clean the faces
Of their children in a mess?

Though I know there are Kleenex tissues
To wipe up spills and tears,
Think how handy mother had it
Back in those former years.

That apron was so versatile,
Its purpose couldn't be weighed;
It carried green beans from the garden
And fresh eggs the hens had laid.

Then when the rain began to fall
Mother spread that apron like a fan
And chased the chicks right in the coop.
They understood her plan.

In the morning around the table,
to read the Bible before we ate,
We heard footsteps from above
And knew that she was late.

Little sister would run to mother's lap
Where the apron wrapped around her feet.
She could feel our mother's love
Because that love was now complete.

Then we would bow our heads,
Thanking God for health and food,
For the family that sat
Around the table. All seemed good.

Now it really doesn't matter
Whether you wear apron, slacks or dress,
Just be sure the love of Jesus
Is what you represent.

Our Church Steeple
Betty Muhlnickel

O steeple tall and steeple bright,
The sunlight shows your stately height.
It brings to mind the church below.
It gives a warm and lasting glow
To see it there amidst the snow.

My mind does wander back to long ago
When another light shone bright above . . .
And shepherds saw and followed it
To the stall of a baby wrapped in swaddling clothes.

O steeple tall, O steeple bright,
Why can't we always keep in sight
That wondrous feeling of awe and love,
And share with others, no matter whom,
No matter where, that wonderful feeling
When first we saw that baby small
And stood in awe!

O steeple tall, O steeple bright,
I'm so grateful for your church below.

*My husband and I lived just about two blocks away from our Brethren
Church. In the winter when the leaves were off the trees, we could see
this church steeple from our living room. One day as I looked out at this
scene, these thoughts came to me and I sat down and wrote this poem.*

The Journey
Sandra Neilson

A new life unfolds,
A child happily roams the family farm.
She's a daughter, a sister, a grandchild,
A schoolgirl, enchanted with learning.
She's a young girl in love,
Then a wife, and a mother,
A working woman
Rearing her children,
Hoping all their dreams come true.

Now a parent alone
Raising her children,
She seeks a new beginning.
College, a job beckons
Her garden blooms abundantly.
Through trials and tribulations
Life goes on,
Life is good.
Her dreams are coming true.

Through life's journey
They share many glad moments,
Some sad ones, too.
Many prayers are said,
For family and friends.
They grow together.
Then the children take wing
And fly on their own
Seeking their dreams.

The house is now empty.
The first time she's lived alone.
The night winds howl,
The house creaks

With fear of the unknown.
But as dawn rises
She realizes she's not alone.
God's beside her,
Fulfilling their dreams.

September in the Country
Erma Yoder

Listen to summer's good-byes and enjoy her grand finale.
Fading walnut leaves
whirl and spin in the breeze
on their way to the tired grass below.
Tickleweed casts a subtle pink hue,
waiting for its freedom in the wind.
Wisps of morning fog hang lazily in the air.
Steam rises from the meandering creek
where a heron, with perfect balance
freezes on one scrawny leg,
watching for breakfast to swim by.
Tall pokeweed flaunts its deadly purple radiance.
Goldenrod's bright plumes dance and reach and wave.
Bluebirds and finches call to one another
and cardinals sing their "cheer."
Bees urgently hum and gather
while butterflies bask, kiss, flutter
and dragonflies flit, dart, click.
Crickets and cicadas strum the night,
while grasshoppers scuttle in half flight.
Geese fly overhead in noisy formation,
As white clouds scud across a cobalt sky.
Fresh crisp mornings, warm sunny days,
chilly evenings earlier each day,
are all reminders of the season's change ahead.
Yellow daisies punctuate the tall spent grass.
As dusk settles,
tree toads begin to squeak, their calls reach a crescendo
in the half-moon night.

Part 3: The Judges
Contest Sponsor

The Judges

Poetry

Shari Wagner, Westfield, Ind., has an M.F.A. in Creative Writing from Indiana University and a BA from Goshen College. Her poems have been published in various literary magazines, including North American Review (forthcoming), The Christian Century, Southern Poetry Review, Indiana Review, Black Warrior Review, and in the anthology, A Cappella Mennonite Voices in Poetry (University of Iowa Press). In 2005, Cascadia Press published her first collection of poems, Evening Chore. She has been awarded multiple fellowships from the Arts Council of Indianapolis and the Indiana Arts Commission, and, twice, her poems have been nominated for a Pushcart Prize. Her husband, Chuck, is a high school English and writing teacher. They are the parents of two daughters.

Essays

Leonard Beechy, Goshen, Ind., teaches English at Northridge High School in Middlebury, Ind. He has academic degrees from Goshen College and Notre Dame University. He is an alumnus of Associated Mennonite Biblical Seminary, Elkhart, Ind. Leonard has published works of short fictions, poetry and the study book The Meaning of Tough: Wealth and Power, in the Closer Than a Brother series (Faith & Life Resources). He is a veteran writer of the Adult Bible Study for Mennonite Publishing Network. His wife, Sharon, is an elementary school teacher. They are the parents of two adult daughters. He is a member of an acoustic vocal and instrumental trio called the Schmalzentrubers.

Contest sponsor

Explaining a retirement community to adults can be a challenge. Double that for children. Still, children catch on quickly. For example, at a distribution of hats and mittens donated by seniors to children at the Goshen Boys & Girls Club in 2006, one child responded to the question, "What is Greencroft?" with a quick answer: "My Mom works there," he said. Another said, "It's a place where grandparents live."

They're right. A Greencroft community is a place where people work and live. Most of the residents are able to care for themselves, volunteer, take care of a garden, travel, play games, use the computer, read, attend concerts and classes, exercise and enjoy their hobbies. They have the freedom to try new things, such as paint, play in a string orchestra even if they've never played a string instrument before, or sing in a choir. They like living where they feel safe and know who to call when something needs to be fixed.

Some people who live in a Greencroft community receive help to do things they are unable to do by themselves. Some need the care of nurses, social workers and therapists. Some residents are 100 years old and older. They are happy for friends, old and new. They welcome visits.

More than 1,700 people live in Greencroft-related communities in northern Indiana. These communities include:

- Hamilton Grove, opened in 1922 in New Carlisle, serves 270 residents.
- Greencroft Goshen, founded in 1962 with doors opened in 1967, serves 1,200 residents.
- Southfield Village, South Bend, opened in 2000, serves 120 residents.
- Greencroft Middlebury, opened in 2004, serves 35 residents, with new homes available.
- Oak Grove Christian Retirement Village, DeMotte, opened in 1999, serves 90 residents (currently Greencroft Communities provides management services by contract).

Greencroft Communities serves as the umbrella organization for these affiliated communities. Each community is a not-for-profit entity, with its own board of directors appointed by the Greencroft Communities Board of Directors.

MHS Alliance, in turn, appoints the Board of Directors for Greencroft Communities and provides the connection to the Mennonite Church. People from at least 20 faith traditions make up the resident populations.

Wherever you live, whether in a Greencroft community, in the greater community, or in another state or country, may you be abundantly rewarded through your interactions, and sharing your stories, within your circles of family and friends of all ages.